THE HEARTBROKEN DIARIES

Spousal Loss - Surviving the Early Years

& Grieving Through a Pandemic

by

Lauren Giordano

****

PUBLISHED BY:

Harvest Moon Press LLC

Cover by The Killion Group, Inc.

1. http://www.laurengiordanoauthor.com

Preface:

Three years ago, the life I knew and loved ceased in a heartbeat. A cataclysmic moment I will never be able to forget. No one is more surprised than me to find myself still standing. Still breathing. Still *here*. There have been times over the last three years when I would have said I was greatly disappointed by that fact. Today, I feel differently—most days. Today, I am trying to ascribe meaning to the reasons I am still here. The last year of this overwhelming grief has been slogged through as the world endures a global pandemic. Sadly, there are now so many more of us out here grieving and doing it on our own.

Let me preface this book by saying I am absolutely, one hundred percent NOT an expert on grief. I am only an expert on MY grief. As you are an expert on yours. In the floundering, distracted days after the worst loss of my life, I sought something to clutch onto. Familiar things. Routines. Structure. Something I could fall back on when I was incapable of thinking rationally. Something that would comfort me as I began staggering down a new path, a frightening and achingly lonely journey with no destination. I sought reassurance that the thing I'd feared most wouldn't be the thing that ended up destroying me.

Familiar for me is writing. Writers write. So, for better or worse, I started writing about this. My husband's horrible, unexpected, supremely unfair, premature death. My nightmare, come to life. Documenting the worst moments of my life has been the most excruciating thing I've ever done, aside from actually living these moments. Yet, I couldn't shake the compulsion to continue this journal. At times disjointed, incoherent and rambling, I have tried to go back and edit for clarity to account for the passage of time.

I include a few hindsights, not to change how I felt as I lived this nightmare, but only in the hope of providing insight to things I've learned along the way as I now look back. If it can possibly help someone else suffering through this awful journey, that is my only goal.

I guess I could insert a platitude here -'that which doesn't kill you makes you stronger'. . . blah, blah, blah. But, platitudes don't work with crushing grief. We don't have a choice on strength or endurance. After a loss, we exist because we must. There's not a single moment of this process that I could say I've been grateful to have been selected. There is no person out there who's saying, 'soul crushing grief—yeah, man, sign me up'. Unfortunately, there is no silver lining to be found in these pages. I'm three years in now. For the last year as I've been editing, we have suffered through a global pandemic. I am heartbroken to acknowledge there are now even more of us. More suffering. More loss to bear. I pray for all who are embarking on their journey now. Honestly, I'm not sure this book will help you, but I am hopeful you glean something. Embracing the horror of this situation—walking in grief—and attempting to find a new version of me is the only thing that has gotten me this far. I pray it will work for you, too.

Since I'm doing such a terrible job marketing this book, I should also tell you that my intent in writing it was only to try to save myself. Keep me sane while I figured out how I was supposed to come to grips with such a catastrophic loss. However, should this book actually sell any copies, I will be donating half the proceeds to two charities that have become so precious to me during this nightmarish process. Becoming a humane society foster parent was a breakthrough for me (more about this later). I can honestly say that being a foster mom to two cats helped me bear my grief. Shameless plug: You will learn more about Ginger and Iris if you decide to continue reading.

One of the other causes I continue to support through my fiction sales is on behalf of women's shelters. The pandemic has caused such an uptick in the need for emergency domestic violence services; for the safe harbor of food, clothing and shelter for women and children escaping the abuse and violence in their lives. So, there you have it. If you choose to buy this book and embrace this terrible hand we've been dealt, you will be helping others who are in dire straits of an entirely different sort. While helping others may not make us feel better about the life we're struggling to make sense of, I'd be willing to bet it probably won't make us feel worse.

A little about me: Writing about the grief process is simply what I had to do. It's who I am. A compulsion to try to put into words what this process feels like. Most days when I sat down to write, it ended up being a lot of crying and not much writing. This book was written in snippets. As I continued punishing myself by documenting the horror, I thought it would evolve into something I'd look back on ten years from now and wonder how I ever survived such a traumatic event. If I had been a knitter, I would have knit a scarf that could easily be stretched across an entire city. Compulsive eater? I'd now weigh 700 pounds. (FYI—I don't—but check on me in another year).

In the beginning, I had to write this book on my phone in the notes app, because I couldn't bear the thought of sitting at my computer. For many months I was too scattered to rein in my thoughts. Too distracted to focus. It was hard to sit still. I could only accomplish work in small bites. Each entry is deeply personal, yet as I read it back later, I realized much of what I've gone through has managed to hit on some of the universal aspects of grief—what I suspect we are all going through. If you are reading this, I'm truly sorry for your loss. I believe you will see something of yourself in my entries. I hope in some way that provides a measure of comfort that you are not alone. We are all alone together.

At the very least, I hope this book will serve to lower your expectations of what "normal" is during the grief process. Normal is whatever gets us through each day. Others have gone before us and many others will follow after us.

This journal is my personal trail of breadcrumbs. My struggles. My fears. Feel free to compare notes. I hope it will help you feel less alone. It is a summary of my erratic thoughts and feelings during the worst days of my life. For those who have been forced to join this lonely club, we will all go about the endurance test in different ways. My grief therapy group (more about that later) consists of beautiful, strong women who have suffered the same catastrophic loss. And each of us are handling it differently. Each of us is on our own timetable. Each has different worries, fears and ambivalence about the journey we have been forced to take. Yet, in so many ways, we are all incredibly the same.

Whatever way you are managing your pain is probably the right way for you— unless it involves self-harming behavior. Please don't do that to yourself. I'm here to remind you—we've already been through enough. If you take one nugget from this, it is to not give up. Don't give up on yourself. You are all you've got. You need to take care of yourself. You have people who need you. People (or pets) who rely on you. Someone out there is worried about you. Someone out there still needs you. So, please find the help you need to enable you process this terrible blow. I have included a list of resources at the end that is not all inclusive. Please check your local resources first to find the experts who can help you, especially if you need immediate assistance.

My intent with this book is only to help others—if that is even possible. To provide a sliver of hope, that you too, will survive this. We will exit this long, dark tunnel and at some point, we will begin a new life. We will develop a new normal. I'd be lying if I said I was there yet. But I'm definitely *closer* to it. I continue to work on it. Day by day. That is a drastic improvement over the minute by minute and hour by hour plan I was on in the early days.

We didn't choose this new life, nor can we change what has happened. But we can choose how we're going to manage it. We can choose to reach out. To seek help. To try to make the best of what we have remaining. To embrace the pain. Fair warning: if you're looking for a happy ending like the kind I create for my fictional stories—this is definitely not that book. This one is a some-days-have-fleeting-moments-of-happy, some-days-still-deeply-suck kind of ending. Have I sold you on it yet? Are you on board? Let's go.

Part One Early Days:

Merriam-Webster: Early Days - The beginning period or phase of some entity, trend or phenomenon. That which is too soon to know how something will turn out . . .

Day 1: The night smelled of rain. Thick clouds scuttled, threatening another downpour. I should have recognized that for the omen it was. Naively, I took it as a good sign. The rain was past— making it the perfect weather for the ballgame. But I was wrong. It was the perfect, breezy start to the last evening of my husband's life.

I can't breathe. My mouth goes dry and metallic with fear. My heart is pounding as my daughter's traumatized voice registers in my brain. There is a fear in her face I've never seen before. I know instinctively the next words from her mouth are going to be awful. "Dad collapsed. We have to go. They're getting an ambulance for him." Over the roar in my ears, I hear the crowd cheering a play at first base. The game we were all attending. The good time we were supposed to be having. The smell of rain in the air; the breeze holding it at bay. It should have been a perfect night. Instead, it soon becomes the worst night of my life. The night I will be unable to ever forget. The night I can only pray IS the worst night of the remainder of my life.

Two days earlier, we'd celebrated the 36th anniversary of our first date. Yeah, we were *that* couple. The couple that said 'I love you' pretty much every day. The couple that rarely ever fought, and if we did, it was usually over something stupid. The couple that still loved hanging out together. The couple that still went out to dinner to celebrate 36 years together. To remember that first date when we got stopped by the cops on our way home. We were best friends. As we reminisced about that night, I remember joking—"we'll *easily* make fifty years together! We're only in our fifties." Two nights later, Dan was gone.

I never appreciated the meaning of the word surreal. It's a word we toss around to describe casual situations, but it's really a word that should be reserved for more substantial occasions. The first days after Dan's death were surreal. The first moments were something beyond surreal. Out of body; shocky, panic stricken; frightened to-the-bone. Instantly dehydrated, as though along with my soul, all the fluids in my body had just vaporized. Terrified. For my husband. For me. For our life. The concrete foundation I'd built my world on. An unwavering, rock solid structure I'd been incredibly content to settle upon, growing old and creaky together forever.

We were supposed to have 50 years—easy. We had it all. Love. Comfort. Familiarity. Best Friendship. All gone in a lightning strike. Out of a clear sky. A painfully perfect spring evening. Enjoying the game he loved. There were no rumbled warnings. No black clouds of foreboding. No flash of insight or shiver of warning to tell me my world was about to snap off its axis and tumble, freefalling into a new galaxy I'd never wanted to visit. Now, I'd been transported there against my will. Permanently.

# # #

1 week: You're still gone. I'm starting to believe this whole nightmare is real. Your funeral has been delayed because of Easter. Because HE has risen along with you. If you didn't already know it, Dan, let me tell you, this is the worst Easter I hope to ever experience. The girls are here for the wrong reason. Their boyfriends are here, suddenly looking older than their years. Desperate to support our girls. Cooking food so people can eat. Personally, I've lost my appetite. I'm not sure it will ever return.

Dan would be so proud of them. The boyfriends are the wonderful young men he believed them to be. They are here. Standing ready to assist me, no matter the unpleasantness of the task. Holding my hand at the funeral home as we have to confirm it's really your body lying there so still. The funeral arrangements at church. The songs we should play to *celebrate* you. How will we possibly *celebrate* anything ever again? Yet, the boys are here with brave faces. To help us make terrible decisions about things I didn't imagine we would be dealing with for another twenty years.

It is very comforting having them here. In this house that suddenly feels entirely too big. Dan and I had already had conversations about downsizing our lives. About us being the last people left at the party. But, in case you've forgotten, we were supposed to clean up the mess together. We were supposed to finish the job we started. To end things on a high note before we could finally head off and have some fun together. Before we emptied out these ten rooms. Whittled down several decades of accumulation, together. Now, he's left me to do it all. It was so unlike him. Dan was the cleanup guy. The guy you could count on to help you with whatever mess you faced. He was a furniture mover; truck renter; sweat dripping down his back as he took vacation days to help friends and kids move. How am I supposed to do all this alone?

How will this house feel after the girls leave? After the boyfriends leave? After the houseful of guests? It feels as though my quiet refuge is now exploding at the seams. It feels like I've had to speak more words to more people in the past few days than I've spoken in twenty years. Explaining. Over and over and over. Trying to hold it together. Through the funeral home event, where more people showed up than were at our wedding. And today, at his funeral.

If I hadn't been completely numb to the circus of events, I would have been proud of how many people came to pay their respects to Dan. The place was packed. His friends. Our friends. His coworkers. My coworkers. Young women he'd coached in softball when they were ten years old. So many of our daughters' friends came to support them. My best friends drove 500 miles down to see me. If Dan hadn't died last week, the 40th anniversary crew was supposed to be meeting up in Quebec for a reunion. I should have been flying out today. I've known these four women since we were in grade school. It was the first group trip we'd ever tried to plan since high school. Instead of the excitement of a four-day weekend catching up with old friends, I was at our church burying my 56-year-old husband. Instead of brunch at the Chateau Frontenac, I was asking one of Miranda's friends to move Dan's ashes out to the car for the ride home. I hope I never say those words again. "Can you move Dan out to the backseat of my car?" My daughter's friend looked briefly fearful and then he bravely complied. Ray is now endeared to me forever.

Dan's ashes are heavier than I imagined. Not that I'd ever spent any time wondering about that previously. I lugged him upstairs and set him on the bureau for now. As desperate as I am for this horrible, surreal week to be over. For the guests to finally be gone. I don't want the girls to leave. I don't want the boyfriends to leave. I don't want to stay here alone. I want the five of us to live inside this bubble until the pain becomes more bearable. Even as I type this, I wonder if that day will ever really come. I can't allow my brain to imagine what next week will be like. Without him. The house I've always loved suddenly feels like a silent, judging stranger.

# # #

1.5 weeks: Is This Real? I hate that I used to be a confident person and overnight, I've pretty much become afraid of everything. The future—which seems pretty pointless now. The decisions I've been forced to make. About who I am without Dan's confidence boosting me up. I'm afraid of the vast emptiness staring me down. I'm not sure I want to know who the real me is under this layer of desperation. I'm afraid now of things I'd never imagined before. Of getting sick—because now there'll be no one to take care of me. To make me soup. Make sure I'm alive. I have no one to be my backup. No one to care. When you've been with someone for 2/3 of your life— who are you without that person?

Fear has moved in with me. An unwanted guest I don't know how to get rid of. If I allow it to stay, it will come to rule this house. Mostly, I'm afraid for my beautiful girls losing their dad so damned early. And not just a dad—but a Super Dad. Let's face it. Dan was the perfect dad. He would have been destined for the Dad Hall of Fame. A loving cheerleader who was always in their corner. A man who would do literally anything for them; and did it with a smile; who was always eager to see them; hear from them; talk with them. Text with them on a nearly daily basis.

We were the family everyone would want to be in. Or maybe, the family someone might resent. Because we really, truly loved and liked each other. We were the people who were happy to see each other every day. The damned perfect family. If there's anything to feel lucky about now, it's that we were always fully aware of it. We knew we were lucky. Knew it was special. I hate the word 'blessed' if only because it's so overused. It's now more associated with someone's perfect, humble-braggy Instagram photo. "I'm so blessed" to have this mega mansion, designed in carefully understated hues of ivory, with my perfectly matching blond children and our ridiculously overpriced, matching monogram sweaters (that you should really click the link to). But in this one instance, I will allow it. Our family was blessed. It was really that good. We knew we were fortunate—but without the monograms and muted tones of ivory. And with much cheaper clothing.

You know what's keeping me up at night? I hate that Dan was alone. That he was frightened. That he suffered pain—if only for a few minutes. For the rest of my life, I will question whether it could've been prevented. That maybe if I'd bullied him into taking cholesterol meds it would have bought us an extra decade. That maybe he'd been feeling bad but he didn't mention it to me. That I didn't pick up on subtle signals that are now so obvious.

Looking back on it, he'd been tired lately, but I explained it away with the horrible work stress he'd been under the past year. Dan had complained a couple weeks earlier about his heart fluttering. But when I questioned him, he'd said it was similar to the flutter he got every year during allergy season—once he started taking his allergy pill. Since he'd just started taking them again a few weeks ago, I didn't question it. Now, I wonder constantly. Why didn't I take that as a signal he should finally start seeing a cardiologist? Was I too dismissive of a clear sign? I'm blaming God for taking him too early, but was He sending signs and we just didn't see them? Did he have pains he glossed over? That's kind of a stupid question, because we all have pains that we ignore. We ignore them because we're not expecting to die in the middle of the third inning of a college baseball game on a random Wednesday night.

Was he worried, but trying not to be? Was he just sitting there faking it? Trying to act natural? Was he sick that day at work? His co-workers told me (at the funeral) it was just a normal day. A normal day that ended with my husband dying.

I hate that I'll never eat a hamburger again without thinking I'm poisoning myself. Not that I can eat much of anything. Now, I have to worry about drinking a margarita with friends. Will I stop at only one? Could I end up falling down? Am I weak now? Was I always weak—and it's been a hidden trait because I always had Dan to lean on?

I used to be a person who never dithered on making decisions. I never questioned our love. Or our choices. Now, I find myself questioning everything. Or worse— not knowing. Not having a damn clue. Where do I go? How will I do on my own? Am I a good person? How can I be a good person when I failed him? Am I capable? How will our girls fare? How do I protect the beautiful, unbreakable family I always believed we possessed? When now—we're all shattered in a million tiny pieces. How do shards of your life go back together? When they're pulverized to dust? Can you put dust back together? Or do you just sweep it up and dump it in the bin?

How do we not go astray now? How do we not lose our way when our guiding light has been snuffed out? Dan was our beacon. He was the good one. The cheerful guy who always had a smile. The man faithful to God and our family. He was strong. Reassuring. Always positive. He was the glass half full guy. Now, our glass has been smashed on the floor. I and our girls have been cut to bits by the splintered glass left behind. We're leaking like a sieve. Who will hold us all together? How do I make sure I'm functional for the girls? How do I guarantee I can protect them from more heartbreak when I've already failed in the largest way possible?

# # #

2 weeks: Survival Mode I've been back at work for two days. I'm not sure it was the right thing to do, but I was going crazy all alone in the house. My grief is just as hard at work—maybe worse because I have to face people. The people who come in to comfort me are just as hard as the people who avoid me, too frightened to take the risk of triggering a meltdown. I appreciate both. Because I feel the same way. For a few moments I can sit at my desk and pretend I'm working. I can try to find the focus to complete a single task. When people arrive to check on me, I know I'll soon be crying again. Then I'll spend the rest of the day with no makeup, swollen eyes and a massive headache. Yet, I love them for it. I love that they are sitting in my office crying with me. Some of them didn't know Dan, but most of them did. He was larger than life, even at my work. Twenty years of parties and family events. Everyone knew and liked him.

At home, I'm surrounded by smiling pictures of Dan, yet his essence is gone. Why don't I feel his presence? I realized today that I've never gone longer than a day or two without talking with him. In 36 years we'd never run out of things to say. Now, it's been nearly 2 weeks without hearing his voice. 2 weeks without a text message. An 'I love you'. I really miss you, Dan. Please come back. The calendar is loaded with his scribbles. Appointments. The trip he didn't get to take. Mostly, it's ball games. Dan loved baseball. This weekend, his schedule would've been packed with games. It's good weather, too. He would've been smiling; so eager to get there. He would always get there early. To see batting practice. But mostly to just be outside on a perfect day. Soaking in the ballpark. It makes me smile at first. Then I cry for all the simple joys he's lost. And all the enjoyment I would get from seeing him so happy. How will I feel when I get to the end of this calendar? When there are no more jotted notes? No plans. Nothing on the calendar to remind me of him. What then? Did we ever exist?

Is he happy where he is now? I pray he is. I pray that this supreme anguish has value in trade for losing the life we loved so much. Because without him, the life remaining here doesn't hold much shine. I picture endless days. Can I be happy without him? What kind of happy will it be? Or will I now be living just a placeholder life? Here to bear witness to all Dan won't see. Of all the joys he will miss. Our girls' lives. I need them to be happy again someday. I will work hard to make sure they are. But we really needed him here, too. This was never supposed to be a one-person job, Dan. It was always us. Together. United with a common goal. In my heart I know he didn't want to go yet. He wouldn't leave us unless there was no other choice. But now that he has, I can only do the best I can for both of us.

# # #

3 weeks: Numbness In our big empty house it's hard to come home at night knowing I'll be the only one there. What used to be my sanctuary at the end of a long or stressful day has become somewhat of a prison. I adore this place, the memories and wonderful times it contains, but I wonder how long I can stay in a home meant for a huge family when it's now just me. Consequently, I find myself trying to fill the space with background noise.

First, it was to pretend Dan was downstairs watching baseball from the west coast as I headed off to bed. I used to have a smile on my face, knowing he'd just end up falling asleep down there, likely 20 minutes after I went to bed. But he was always so excited to choose a game from the zillion or so in the sports package. Now, it has started to settle in that he's really gone. He's not on a trip. He's not working late. I can't fool myself any longer. So, instead, I come through the door, wake up the sleeping giant house and break the stillness with music. Dan adored the Alexa the girls gave him for Father's Day last year. Asking it questions; checking the weather, sending messages to the girls and playing music. He played it endlessly. Song after song after song. So now I do, too. Music has become the background noise in my too quiet life. I'll bet Dan never knew you can search the history on it. With technology we can now do anything, including morphing back in time. To the day he was still here issuing orders to Alexa.

I wonder if he knew we used that technology to build his play list for the funeral home. We traced his song history and recreated it to accompany the beautiful slide show the girls created to summarize his life. Happy music to sync with the endless pictures of his smiling face. I only wish we could've heard his voice issuing the orders to Alexa because we really could've used a laugh those first, awful days. As he would issue an order but forget to say 'Alexa'. As he overcorrected and rambled and she told him she didn't understand his request. As he'd try a third time, his voice escalating with his request, until he'd finally swear at her despite it not being her fault. Those tracks would've been funny to hear.

Today, my daughter Chelsea was here. We decided to go through one of his archive boxes. For decades, Dan had been jotting notes and poems and essays and he'd throw them in his box. His "archives", he called them. So, Chelsea and I asked Alexa (nicely) to play Dan's favorite radio station in the background as we tentatively opened the box.

Damned if the first song that started playing was our first dance song from our wedding. Lionel Ritchie. *Stuck on You*. And I burst into tears. Were you here with us, Dan? Did you sit beside us as we poured thru hundreds of scraps of paper? Your old school records? Turns out you saved every card I ever gave you. We read some of them, dating back to 1982. Only months into our relationship. I knew you'd always written poems and short little essays about whatever you were feeling in the moment, but I never knew how much quantity there was. We found stuff dating back to your high school years and essays about how much you loved coaching our girls on their softball teams.

We found the letter you wrote your mom that she'd later returned to you, insisting you save it for your girls. The letter was from your early years in coaching. About a young girl whose mom told you her daughter had never fit in anywhere, but that on your team, she'd finally found a home. Her daughter actually looked forward to attending softball practice. She'd told the mom that she would only ever play for you. The woman had told Dan she was so grateful to him for having such an impact on her daughter's life. We read how you explained to your mom that you viewed coaching as a gift and a responsibility to God to welcome her and do all you could to make her feel wanted on your team.

I've always known your soul, Dan, but I never knew about that conversation. You never shared that note with me. Finding it in his archives made me smile and cry at the same time. It was so typically Dan. Humble and giving and kind to the very end.

For the first time maybe ever, I finally understood why he loved coaching so much. Because the winning never mattered (obviously)!! Their record was horrendous. Over seven years, they were like 10 and 110. But, for him it was about the welcome he extended to all girls. To come out and play and have fun. To feel included. To feel good about something. To make friends and to never feel ashamed about not playing well enough.

The very last thing his coaching was about, was winning games—to several parents' chagrin. Every season, the same parents questioned his coaching ability. His unregimented style. Every season, these same parents were unwilling to sacrifice the endless hours required to coach but remained more than happy to complain about the team's record and why their daughter (who was always a superstar) wasn't playing more. Yet, every season, girls would return to his team. Knowing in advance they'd probably lose most games. Dan was the guy who brought Popsicles to every practice. He bought stacks of washcloths so he could chill them in a cooler and bring them out for the girls to drape on the nape of their neck when it was suffocatingly hot and they were playing a doubleheader. The girls called him Coach Creampuff. He wore that moniker like an Olympic gold medal. I love him so much for that.

# # #

3.5 weeks: The first life insurance check came today. Staring at it, I felt no relief. Only a sense of obligation. Decisions have become much harder now. Weighty. Each one seems critical and foreboding. What is the right decision when I have both short term worries and longer-term obligations? I know what we'd always planned. But, that's all gone. Now, I have to think about me. Which has always been difficult but has grown exponentially more so since Dan upended our plans. How do I know what I want anymore? When every plan we made revolved around an 'us'?

I look at the totals and I can't help wondering— is this all we amount to at the end of our days? Is the sum total of our life merely a number? This much life insurance and that much 401k? Before Dan was gone, those numbers provided us comfort. They powered our dreams. Those numbers reminded us every day the reason why we slog thru the endless weeks and months and years of working. Those numbers were the reason we dragged ourselves out of bed on a cold, rainy Monday and drove thru slush to a job we *liked*, but let's face it—was still just a job. Those numbers were our future. Our dreams of walking beaches together. Dan's dream of spending a month at Red Sox spring training camp. Of babysitting our grandchildren and watching them thrive. Of us finally giving ourselves permission to have so much more fun.

Now, they are just numbers. Calculated. Reassuring—if only because I won't be left out on the street. Ultimately, they are meaningless figures on a page. Empty promises of dreams never to be achieved. They are without a soul. Until I someday figure out what those numbers are going to mean to me—going it alone. What they mean to our girls—who may have to help me someday if I don't plan wisely now.

# # #

Hindsight 1: Music. My grief process rekindled my appreciation for classical music. I'd always loved attending concerts. Growing up in Massachusetts, I was a big fan of the Boston Symphony Orchestra and their summer home of Tanglewood. However, in the early months of inconsolable grief, my house was so unbearably quiet. Yet, the popular music I'd always loved became too jarring to listen to. I was confused and disoriented. Music with lyrics suddenly became too much for me to hear. It became noise instead of pleasure. One day, I just asked Alexa to play classical music and eventually, orchestras. The change was immediately calming. I had noise in the background of my new, awful life, but instead of agitating me, it helped me start to quiet. I could feel myself unclenching. Some pieces just spoke to me. I discovered that classical music was the soundtrack to my grief. How could any piece of music sound *exactly* as I felt? Yet so often it did. So, if I was crying anyway, I may as well have a score for it.

On good days, classical music would make me smile. Some were uplifting and would help carry my mood. Or prevent it from spiraling too far down. Now, much to my kids' chagrin, it's on in my house all the time. Even in the car, I'm usually listening to classical music. Those calming, dulcet-toned NPR radio hosts describing the next symphony I would be hearing. So unclenching. I wish I could tell you this relaxation method will improve your tolerance and driving behavior on the road, but alas, it hasn't done that for me.

Hindsight 2: Decision making: This is me chiming in from the almost-three-year point: What the experts say about not making big decisions too soon has merit. Although I could just as easily argue that literally every decision you make in the immediacy of your loved one's death is going to be difficult. But Widow's Fog is real. Terror and grief are real. These emotions do a number on you and impact how you react to everything. When I review what I wrote at the 1, 2 and 3 week point, I am floored to be reminded how shaky and vulnerable I was. Not that I'm normally brilliant or anything, but I can honestly say I was not of sound mind at the three-week point. I likely wasn't completely rational at the six-month point. But let's face it. Some decisions must be made during that period of extreme vulnerability.

Do I have to pay for the funeral? Yes. Do I need to pay my mortgage this month? Yes. Do I need to pay off my house tomorrow? No. There are bills you need to pay to continue functioning. To keep the lights on. To keep from being evicted. Those immediate decisions are the ones to focus on. Set aside everything else. All the 'big' decisions can wait. Seriously. Now is the time to conserve your energy. You're overwhelmed. Give yourself permission to wait on anything that isn't a deal breaker. Take a breath and set them aside. Allow yourself this gift.

For the decisions that can wait: Find someone trusted who can talk you through each situation. Preferably someone with knowledge of the subject matter. At the very least, find someone who can be neutral. This is not the time for you to be overwhelmed by people who may be *too* close to your decision to be helpful. Nor do you want someone who may have an agenda about your money. Our situation is bad enough. We don't need family infighting or people who think "they know best"; who want to take over "to help you". This is your situation. Your life. You don't need battles for control right now.

Going forward, you need to feel comfortable with the decisions you make. You may as well start now. Learn to get comfortable saying no.

Try to help yourself by prioritizing. Determine the immediacy of the decision. Does it need to occur now? These are the decisions you can discuss with the trusted person. For the decisions that can wait, start looking for the knowledge you need. A financial planner (or accountant or tax person or benefits person at work) who can walk you through your options. If you don't know anyone, ask a friend. Get references.

Ultimately, I ended up meeting with three advisors—because I am cursed with being methodical. All suggested different courses of action. None of them were wrong. Just different spins on the same allocation of limited resources. Each one raised issues I hadn't thought of. I can already hear you thinking— *but I'm already so overwhelmed*. Let me just say, I was too, at first. Let's face it, it doesn't take much to become overwhelmed in the early days. I met with these advisors over a 3-4 month period. Then I digested what I learned from each one. And then I sat on it for a while. Eventually, I was able to admit that diverse ideas were a good thing. Despite their ideas resulting in my having more choices to mull over, I was taking my time on the actual decision-making process, right? Hopefully, what will happen is one or a few ideas may speak to you. Or spark ideas of your own. Or match up with something you'd already been leaning into. I'm in the camp of I'd rather work with more information than less.

Listen to a few experts. They will all have different opinions. I learned things that never would have crossed my mind. So, it's worth keeping an open mind and hearing their suggestions. Digest the information from each person and then just sit on it. Mull over what you learn from each expert. Eventually, you can start to incorporate pieces of information into the picture you've begun sketching. The possibility picture that begins to emerge from the ashes of your old life. What are you worried about? What do you wish for? Whatever you find yourself dwelling on is probably a good place to start your planning. If it's keeping you up at night, it's probably important. Even when we can't really think coherently, our subconscious is probably nudging us in a specific direction. Let that be your guide as opposed to all the sales pitches.

Whatever you've been left with—that's what you have to work with. Whether it's a million dollars or it's nothing— if you're like me, we never planned for there to be only one income left at this stage of the game. I had real fears over whether I could support myself with just my income. Would I be able to pay all the bills? Later, my worry became- will I be able to help my daughters? Would there be money for weddings someday? Will I ever be able to retire? We all have our personal list of concerns. Allow someone to help you muddle through it. Find someone you trust. If you don't know anyone, consider consulting a fee-only planner so you aren't taken advantage of when your guard is down. Let's face it, we're vulnerable for a very long time after our loss. At the very least, we should acknowledge that weakness and plan around it.

Among all the grief books I read, I also read Suze Orman's book on retirement (details in the resource section). I was pleasantly surprised to discover her advice was in essay format which offered small chunks of information. This was helpful to me because since Dan died, I still have a hard time focusing for long periods. Orman's advice is delivered in digestible bites. It was truly insightful (and kind of inspiring). Orman takes the view that it is never too late to help yourself. To change course, develop a plan, etc.

When you get a late start, it's easy to believe it's hopeless and you'll never have (insert dream here). A home. A vacation. College. Retirement. Orman has a readability style I appreciated. No matter what level of financial knowledge you have, her explanations break things down to an understandable level. She has published dozens of books on personal finance for all age groups. I'm sure there are other financial writers out there who are just as great, but I haven't read them yet. Just before the pandemic hit and shut everything down, I was fortunate to attend a retirement planning class at my local community college. It's part of my continuing attempt to absorb information that will help me make critical decisions as I move forward alone.

# # #

4 weeks: The 'Why' Days The girls visit more often now. One of the hardest aspects of grief is the isolation. With our girls far away, I feel the distance more than ever before. Though I am ecstatic when they visit, the void becomes a yawning chasm once they leave again. I am acutely conscious on the last day— of the ticking clock that will whisk them away from me in a few short hours. Though we are all thinking the same thing, we leave it unspoken. "I'll be back again soon, Mom. Only two more weeks."

Part of me feels bad they are so worried about me they feel they must visit so often now. Yet, I have to admit that I desperately need to see them. I hate that I have become their burden. One more thing they are forced to worry about. We have officially reversed roles. I have become the toddler being dropped off at preschool. When they leave, they hesitate. Waiting uncomfortably. Likely praying I don't burst into tears before they embark on their long drive back. We all try to prevent triggering the domino effect of grief. The dam holding it all back as the veneer slowly begins to crack. Until the flood waters tumble over the walls again.

We all worry more now. We have anxiety about driving. About accidents. About any terrible thing that could possibly tear apart our already ravaged family. Because the worst has happened to us. We are now one of *those* families. The ones you read about and say 'thank God that couldn't happen to us'. But it finally has. *Happened to us.* The glorious bubble we resided inside for more than 3 decades finally popped. Which means it could happen again. And all of us fear it, as we try desperately not to think about it.

I eat dinner alone every night in Dan's leather chair. Eating at a table that seats six is no longer something I can face anymore. I choke down food because I know I must eat as I continually wonder how this giant mistake has occurred. I wonder how I would've spent that last hour with him if I'd only known. Instead of meaningless chit chat as we waited in line for a hamburger at the game. What would I say? I try to appreciate all the years we had together—all the happiness—but instead, all I feel is screwed. Denied time with the best person I've ever known. As terrible people still walk the earth, the light of my life is gone.

Why was there no warning shot fired across the bow? No second chance? No 'little' heart attack first? That warning sign would have terrified us but would have forced changes. To his diet. He exercised like a fiend, out of this very fear. A heart attack. So, there wasn't much more he could have done on that front. He was strong and healthy—or so we believed.

If he'd had even 10 more years, he would've received the satisfaction of seeing our girls' milestones. Weddings. Babies. Even then— 10 more years would have *still* been too young. Now, our girls will have a gaping hole in their lives. Their important events. What should be their happiest days will instead be bittersweet. He won't be there to walk them down the aisle. They'll be missing the proudest grandfather on the sidelines—cheering them on and telling them what amazing parents they are. It's just so wrong.

Why did God choose Dan? Why did he destroy us? Were we too happy? Was I too cocky about how good our life was? We tried to live a grateful, humble life. We appreciated each other every day. We never took our relationship for granted. As careful as we were to respect our good fortune, it has still been snatched away. I find myself feeling worse each day; not better. Not comforted that he's in a better place. Because I am stuck in this terrible lonely life without him.

# # #

1 month: Fog & Pain A month has officially passed. Some days are better than others. Brief pockets of normal in days of doubt and uncertainty. I'm no longer sure about anything, so I cling to the familiar. I crave life to be normal again, despite knowing normal doesn't exist for me anymore. There is only what might hopefully become a tolerable substitute for normal.

To get away from the house on the one-month mark, I drove up to DC to see the girls, who were both briefly in the same place for the weekend. And the boyfriends. We had a wonderful time, despite being hyper aware of the time marker we were trying to forget. To avoid talking about it, lest one of us break down in tears while we strolled along the Potomac. A beautiful day spent with the people I love most, yet I still had an unshakable heaviness in my chest. I stayed in a beautiful B&B, yet only slept a few hours. If I didn't already know it, I learned you can't escape your grief. You can't outrun the overwhelming sadness swamping you. You just have to wade thru it and hope it will someday lessen. It's not as though I want to forget. I just want Dan back. I want what I can't have.

The questions are still a litany of unknowns, first of which is how long will it take my heart to accept it? How long before my being alone won't be a terrifying substitute for the life I had? How much time has to pass before I won't miss the girls as soon as I leave them? Until I don't want to cling onto them for dear life or wrap us in bubble wrap so no one else can get hurt or sick. How long before I stop wishing I had everyone living back at home? As though if the house was full and noisy I somehow wouldn't miss Dan? How long before I stop feeling guilty for surviving without him? How much time has to pass before I don't relive his last night *every night*? Until I stop feeling as though I dropped the most important ball I could ever carry?

Why didn't I know he was in pain? Why did my mind scurry to the safe place? To the 'it's a pulled muscle in his shoulder' place? To the 'it can't possibly be a heart attack' place? Was he scared? Did he know it was bad? Was he afraid to tell me? Did he leave us because he knew? Was he protecting us? Or just frightened out of his mind?

Why didn't I follow him when he got up that last time to "walk it off"? How long will I experience this tremendous sense of remorse? Most days it feels as though God is punishing me. For not paying attention. For not recognizing I was losing you right before my eyes. God, where are you? I need you to tell me it wasn't my fault; yet in my heart I know He can't. It's likely that nothing could be done. But I could've been with him. I could've been holding his hand. I could've been telling Dan how much I loved him. Instead, he was alone. With strangers working on him—when we finally realized he'd been away from his seat too long. How do I learn to live with that? What if I make that mistake again?

# # #

5.5 weeks: I'm officially despondent now. I have tried to be strong. I've kept my chin up. I've smiled at work. Nodded that I'm doing okay. I've voiced the platitudes other people need to hear from me. God needed him. The girls and I will come out stronger. He wouldn't want us to be sad. But let's face it. This new normal— coming home to a too big, too empty house— really sucks. Everyone's gone back to their normal; their busy lives; their families. But my life is forever changed.

I find myself getting easily frustrated by things that in "old normal" never bothered me. Yet, I am grateful for all the little things that now resonate in my too quiet life. The wonderful neighbor who retrieves my trash can each week when she gets hers. The same wonderful neighbor who has started prodding me to go walking with her in the evenings. Two nights in a row, I had someone to talk with while getting some much-needed exercise. When a thunderstorm dashed our plans last night, I missed that time together.

I am physically exhausted each night, yet when I sleep— if I sleep— it is restless and filled with the last images I have of Dan. His worried face. I'd chalked it up to fatigue; yet I believe now that he knew differently. Why wasn't I paying attention? Worried about the most important person in my life? We all have little aches and pains. No one believes their spouse is going to die on a random Wednesday night, but why didn't I sense the catastrophe that was crashing down? Why did he leave us to "walk it off"? Did he sense the unfolding tragedy? Was he trying to protect us? Run from the pain closing in? The next time I saw him, he was on a gurney; oxygen mask over his face; but I could tell he wasn't breathing.

The next time was at the hospital. After. When everything that could have been done had been tried. Unsuccessfully. I held his hand, not cold yet, but so still. Not squeezing mine back. A huge hand, that for 36 years, I could count on for anything I needed. Anything I wanted. Anything that was within his power to give me. I am alone now. There is no one out there who will miss me. Worry about me. Text me in the middle of the day. No one who will wonder if my flight arrived safely. Whether I'm happy. Or sad. Or had a bad day. And I feel lost. Adrift in a new normal I want no part of.

As I sit here crying for the 38th day in a row, I am consumed with sadness, regret and fear about what lies ahead. Because if there's one thing more awful than not knowing your future, it's knowing it. Knowing I must go on for God knows how long— without the single person I absolutely can't do without. I am now a stranger in a sea of friends. The fifth wheel at any gathering. I am alone. And I don't see how I will ever be able to bear this.

# # #

7 weeks: I frightened the girls tonight. I attended a work dinner, so my phone was off. I wasn't thinking they might be looking for me. Three hours later as I was leaving the hotel, I discovered numerous text messages; increasing in worry level as time went on. I immediately called to reassure them I was fine. But their stress level quickly reminded me of the strange, new landscape we inhabit. The one where bad things can happen. Have happened. To us. Not strangers. Not people we read about in the faraway "elsewhere". But here. Now.

We are all painfully aware that life can change in an instant. When I drive the two hours to visit our older daughter, there is both eagerness and worry. Will I make it safely? Or will they be shattered once more? When my youngest drives the 5 hours it takes for her to get to me, I'm vigilantly aware of the clock. Of where she should be— if everything is going well. I want to see them constantly, yet I worry I am statistically exposing them to more danger on the road.

Will it always be this way? I think of my life now in terms of "I can't die yet because I haven't updated the will". I can't die yet because Dan's 401k hasn't rolled over. I need to get it in my name so I can make sure the girls are listed as my beneficiaries. I need to create a new power-of-attorney because the one Dan and I both signed in 1987 is no longer valid. One thing I'm proud of, in spite of all this sadness? That we had the gumption to actually *have* a power of attorney in 1987. In 1987, Dan was twenty-five and I was twenty-three. One thing we did right: we always had a will. Even when we had nothing. We continued over our lifetime together to update that will every five years or so and especially after we had the girls.

I still need to think about a medical directive— feeling both relief once it's done and raw panic that I will be damaging my daughters' psyche by making them responsible for those decisions. I need their names on everything, so if the worst happens, their trauma will hopefully be lessened by knowing everything is in order. As though heartache can somehow be lessened by my superlative organizational skills. But when it's all you have to work with, I feel the obsessive need to tidy things up for them.

In seven weeks, my life is now divided between grief and red tape. When I'm not crying, I'm on the phone trying to figure out why everything takes so long. I'm writing meticulous notes because the fog shrouding my brain makes me forget things—as soon as they happen. The life insurance company that won't pay. The 401k that won't answer basic questions until it's "officially" transferred to me. Really, Fidelity? What do you think will happen if you tell me what the money is invested in? Is that really classified information?

Whether it's a pre-tax account or a Roth? You can't tell me that much? So I could, in the ridiculous month-long wait, open the appropriate account to receive those funds? Focusing on minutiae affords me brief pockets without grief. When I can almost forget why I'm on the phone in the first place. Oh yeah. My husband is dead. And the tears start falling again.

# # #

Hindsight: Money Stuff: Handling all the life insurance, 401ks, health insurance (or COBRA), your home, cars, bank accounts and a million other things would be a massive undertaking when your brain is fully functioning. Trying to do all this when we're grieving is about as close to hell as one can get. However, it all must be done. I tried to tackle my list one line at a time. Each day I would summon the energy and patience to tackle one item on my list. It took months. It will take you months. Some days I accomplished nothing. But, the list won't go away until we tackle it. We have to keep chipping away at it.

Some of the most aggravating and time-consuming tasks were the least important. It probably took seven calls and three visits to switch the cable bill into my name. I finally had to drive there and show them the death certificate, just for the privilege to keep paying their overpriced, ridiculous bill. If I ever completely lose it one day, it's going to be in the lobby of the cable company. And since I don't own a gun, it will probably be me, brandishing an old softball bat as I go berserk bashing in their computer screens. You heard it here first, folks. When you see it on TV, you can say "oh, yeah—that's got to be Lauren."

Another serious topic: Take the time to have a new will drawn up. Seriously. If you have young children, I can think of nothing more critical than who you would want raising them. How you would provide for them financially. If you can't afford an attorney, you can find sites online that will draw up a basic will. However, the $ 300 to $ 600 you might spend with an attorney is money so well spent. The peace of mind alone is worth that price. We probably tweaked ours two or three times during our girls' growing-up years.

Our first guardian was Dan's sister. She's a wonderful person and loves our girls. But very early on, she moved three thousand miles away. We had to have the conversation of where would our girls feel most safe and cared for in the event of a tragedy? Meaning – what would *least* disrupt their lives in the catastrophic event of losing both parents? You need to have this conversation, if only with yourself. Without a will and without a guardianship drawn up, a court will decide what to do with your assets—the most precious of them being your children. If you don't have kids, what about your pets? Wouldn't you want to determine what happens to them? Otherwise, someone else will.

# # #

8 weeks: Bugs and Scones Tonight there was a thunderstorm. An ominous, scary clouds, thunder rumbling; wind howling through the eaves sort of storm. The kind that vibrates through you, making you wish you were out in the thick of it— and also makes you cower, grateful to be safe inside. Lightning flashed and the lights flickered. Normally, this is my kind of storm. The kind where you curl up on the couch and listen to it. Watch it out the windows, awed by Mother Nature's fury. Tonight, I was afraid. And I realized . . . I just can't be. I don't have that luxury. Because there's no one here with me. Dan's not here to laugh with. To gather candles and flashlights. He's not here to joke about my cooking and how the power going out is actually a *great* thing. He's not here to remind me that the claustrophobic darkness isn't creepy. It's time for us to chat. To appreciate the quiet.

Will everything I've ever enjoyed be changed now? Or like my husband being gone, is it just one more sucky, awful thing I'll be forced to get used to? I guess underneath everything— the sadness, the loneliness, the aching grief of missing Dan, underneath all of it, lies fear. That I'm alone. And probably always will be. That he's truly gone and I'll never see him again. Never hear his voice or hear him laugh. See him smile. What if I start to forget that smile? What if, when I ask myself 'what would Dan do?' I suddenly don't know the answer? When I thought I knew everything about him. When I thought I knew everything about me. When I was so damned certain about us. Will I grow to love thunderstorms once again? Can I learn to love being alone? I don't know. I don't know anything anymore. And that's the worst kind of fear I can imagine.

So, I've dealt with storms and alarms going off. With the arduous task of starting to clean out Dan's things. Which is a difficult confirmation that he's not coming back. Stacking up his clothes. Piling them into Goodwill bags. But—being unable to actually move them from the house. It's like admitting defeat. In a battle I never had a fighting chance. A sneak attack that took him away before we could say goodbye.

Since Dan left, I've had to deal with an ant infestation in the kitchen. Twenty years in this house and we rarely dealt with ants. But Dan's gone a couple weeks and all hell is breaking loose in this stupid house. I am facing an ant-pocalypse of biblical proportions. Like—if I could put the house up for sale in the next five minutes, I'd think hard about it. Instead, I called the pest company. In a near hysterical pitch, I heard myself demanding (shrieking) they come out *tomorrow* or I was going to lose it. Note to self: that ship had already sailed. I'm sure their scheduler was not thrilled to be dealing with a shrieking nutcase customer, but those ants were crawling all over my kitchen. The counters. The walls. The gorgeous scones I splurged on. I rarely eat anything these days. Yet, I'd actually been looking forward to eating those fucking scones. I had big plans for them.

The royal wedding was this weekend. Meghan and Harry. I got up—voluntarily—at 5 am to settle in with tea and *scones*. How often do we get to see a royal wedding? It's a historic event. I wanted to be full-on British for just a single day. I'd purchased special tea. It was going to be amazing. I set my alarm. I rolled out of bed. It was finally something I was looking forward to. Something that would make me smile.

Instead, I discovered ants at the commercial break at 7:15 am. Hundreds of them. Crawling all over my beautiful scones. And the counter. I missed part of the ceremony while I was blasting the countertop with bleach—and crying for an entirely new reason.

Now, I'm forced to admit the ant episode has put me off scones—possibly for life. The ant guy was very understanding the following Monday when I met him for my emergency lunch break pesticide bombing. He's probably dealt with lots of unstable women in his line of work.

In some ways I feel strong because I've endured 56 days without Dan here. I've gotten thru one full day without crying, so I guess that's a small measure of success. But, in other ways I feel as though I've completely lost my confidence. I feel exposed. Weaker than I ever realized I could be. I've lost the sturdy, centered independence I had before. Was that ever really me? Or was I like that because I had the security of being tethered to a rock solid husband?

Grief is isolating. At eight weeks, people at work probably feel as though it's been a long time. Yet for me, it hits each day in different ways. Each one heartbreaking. While I don't feel as overwhelmed as I did early on, in some ways it's worse now. Reality has started to sink in. *This* is my new life. A good day for me is not completely losing it at work. A good night is taking a walk with my wonderful neighbor so the time I have to spend alone is shorter. Two nights this week it rained at walk time, making those nights unbearably long. I ended up pacing the four miles through my house, lap after lap, just to burn off the anxiety I could feel building inside me. Those nights I felt like a pressure cooker heating up. Like I possibly might explode.

Occasionally, I have a night like tonight, dinner and a movie with a thoughtful friend who checks in frequently. A rare night when I have fun and we laugh. But, as I drive home to tell Dan all about it, he's not here. As I wander empty rooms, I want to know the future. I want it all to go faster— so I can get to the place where I can just *know* how it will end. Where I'm heading. What becomes of me. How the girls have adjusted. But there's really no outrunning this. Grief is a one man show. It's lonely. And right now, I fear it's permanent. Because I really don't want to move on. I want Dan back. I want a do-over. It's selfish to say this, but I truly never imagined this as our ending. I never imagined being a widow at 54. I never fathomed this awfulness happening to us. I was so wrong.

# # #

9 weeks: Weddings I've learned it is actually possible to cry for 63 days in a row. That's a slight exaggeration— I think I've had two days where I was either too tired to cry, or one day when I managed to forget for an evening. I try to keep busy. Incredibly busy, just to make the hours pass so I don't sit here wallowing.

Monday night, I looked for Dan at the airport as I returned from a trip. He would always be there in the airport lobby, waiting for me whenever I was flying home from somewhere. His routine was that he would pretend he didn't see me; all while standing there with a big grin his face. I flew out on Friday for a wedding and had to drive myself to the airport. Dan would have taken me, despite my stupidity in booking a 6:45 am flight. He would have complained about getting up at 4 am; but then he would have insisted that he really, really wanted to drive me there at 5 am. That it wouldn't be out of his way (it was); that he *wanted* to get in to work early. Then he would've been there waiting Monday night; eager to lug my too heavy bag out to our car. Alone now, this first of many times to come, I could barely lift my bag into the trunk because I'd volunteered to bring some of my daughter's stuff back with me. She was limited to a carry-on on her flight back to Pittsburgh, so I took all her heavy stuff with the promise to ship it to her when I got home.

I flew to Texas for a wedding. It was beautiful and joyful. And so ungodly hot. My first experience at a Jewish wedding. The rabbi was a delightful woman with a beautiful voice. Most of the ceremony was in Yiddish, but she would translate the prayers and sentiments into English. Since the groom's side was mostly Jewish, the answering prayers were a harmony of voices almost chanted back at her. The outdoor evening service was beautiful and mystical. It gave me goose bumps. Even though Dan would never have travelled there with me because he hated flying; I still missed him. The rabbi started the service with a prayer for those not with us and for those who had departed. For those she claimed were now among the stars overhead. Shining brightly down on us. Were you there, Dan? Is that where you reside now? Because if that's the case, it's pretty ironic because you always had such a fear of heights. Are you really looking down on us? Because if you are, I don't feel you. And I truly thought I would.

One thing that hit me while I was away on this trip is that I've lost my champion. I was standing in my hotel room; a few hours before my daughters would arrive, and I realized there was no one out there worrying about me. No one wondering whether I got to Austin safely. I've lost my person. The one who thinks I'm great. Who thinks I'm perfect just the way I am. The one who accepted all my flaws unconditionally. The one who would defend me no matter what. I've lost that faith and love and loyalty. Having to acknowledge its gone now is almost unbearable to live with.

The selfish part of me expected to have Dan's love for so much longer. Seeing my daughter's best friend with her new husband—just starting out. So happy. Their whole lives ahead of them. It made me miss Dan so much more. I don't know how to get through the next twenty years alone. With no partner. With no one to wonder whether I arrived safely. To text me to just say hi. To care that I caught a cold on the trip. It's all the little things I miss. The things that just made me happy I had found my person. The little things are what add up to meaning in life. Those things are gone now. And I don't know how to face a future without them.

# # #

Father's Day: Though we desperately tried to ignore the holiday this year, I couldn't help jotting a few notes about what Dan was like with the girls. He was always present. He texted them a few times a day, whether he had news to share or not. He was a joyful supporter of all they did. They could count on him for congratulations, best wishes, love and joy. He was the 'Happy Thursday' text guy. Always thinking of them. He'd adjusted pretty well to our girls growing up. Becoming beautiful, smart, independent young women. Yet, he still sought ways to be helpful. To feel needed—by smart girls who could do most things on their own.

I was thinking about the Seinfeld episode where Elaine is explaining to the guys that a man's naked body is like a jeep. Its utilitarian; it's reliable. "It gets you where you need to go."

Since our girls were young, their dad has been the guy who took care of everything. Not because they couldn't do it, but because he felt it was his job. He was the all-in parent from the moment each of them arrived. Diaper changing; walking the floors at night; story-reading; drive-30-miles-from-work because one of his daughters forgot her lunch type of dad. Back-breaking moves into and out of dorms, apartments and then more apartments through six years of overlapping college and grad school years, first jobs (and the few years beyond) multiplied by two daughters.

Nothing was ever too much for his little girls. So, flash forward twenty years and we now had two fully grown, smart, talented, fully independent daughters. But they lived far away; Chelsea is thankfully only 100 miles away; but Miranda ended up over 300 miles away. Chelsea was basically the daughter who kept her dad sane. She always checked in a few times a week and we would see her every six weeks or so. Miranda became our long-weekend daughter when she moved to Pittsburgh. We would head out to her twice a year and she tried for twice a year to come home (which is amazing when you consider she has a full life; a boyfriend; a demanding job, pets, etc.).

For her poor father, the trips out to Pittsburgh always seemed to revert him back to 20-yrs-ago dad. As though our grown daughter was too young to be on her own. On trips to her city, Dan would feel the need to make up for 6 months of NOT protecting her. Of not taking out her trash, of not putting together a desk. Of not pumping her gas. Of not reminding her incessantly about walking to her car at night in the big city. And how had she possibly been doing those things without him there? This always drove Miranda—the fully capable daughter we've raised—a little nuts. Comments like "I knoooooow, Dad combined with an eye roll thrown in or with jokes about Dan being Captain Obvious. But, try explaining the art of compulsive over-caring to a fully capable daughter. And you're left w the Seinfeld naked guy/jeep comparison.

Dan was utilitarian. Always reliable. He was the trash manager. The errand runner. The pump-your-gas guy. The guy who got your car inspected. His helpful dad motor still ran, even though the journey was mostly over. That engine didn't want to shut down. It was the old faithful engine that would still rattle a few minutes after you removed the key from the ignition. Knocks and pings and all. Had he lived, Dan would have kept that engine running until the girls were in their fifties. His seventy-five-year-old engine still rattling, long after the jeep had been retired. Long after his job was over. What we all wouldn't give now to hear him making Captain Obvious statements. It's one of the things we miss most about him.

# # #

12 Weeks: Trying Too Hard I had what hindsight would suggest was my first panic attack this week. At the eleventh hour, I was forced to bail on my company's summer outing. Our corporate outing was being held at the ballpark where my husband died three months ago. Dan used to love that night at the ballpark. The picnic. The ballgame. The free beer. The flitting about, talking to all of my co-workers as though they were his own. After twenty years, Dan knew all of them almost as well as I did. He was always the one urging me to mingle. Talk to people. He was definitely the social half of our duet. The guy who showed up in more pictures than me. He would have his picture taken every year with the team's mascot—a big grin on his face. God, I miss all that exuberance. Life is so damned quiet now.

In the weeks leading up to the event, I'd insisted (foolishly) I could return to the venue—maybe not to watch a game, but at least I could help out with the dinner. Assist with the employee awards. The gift basket giveaway. Yet, as the weeks crept up on me, I sensed a flicker of anxiety in the pit of my stomach. A flicker that eventually became a weight of dread as the day drew closer. Then, the flashbacks started—racing me back to that night . . . only a few weeks after they'd finally begun to recede from my brain. My husband had collapsed and died in that ballpark. How in holy hell could I be OK going back there less than three months after it happened?

My co-workers had worried all along that it might be too much for me. But I kept insisting I would be fine. The day before the event, as I slowly descended into basket case mode, I finally admitted I couldn't handle it. That maybe, I might never be able to handle it. So many people had stopped by my office—their faces etched with concern, instinctively knowing what I had been stubbornly refusing to accept. "Are you *sure* you want to go? No one expects you to do this. Are you really sure?" And of course, I wasn't sure. On the inside, I was falling apart. But I nodded, like the good soldier I've always been. The diligent employee for more than twenty years. Desperate to move past the catastrophic loss I'd just experienced. The body blow I was still reeling from. Because I didn't want to be THAT person. The one who needed coddling. Catering to.

I didn't want any attention on me. Yet, in the end, I was causing attention. People were worried about me. And I ended up bailing on the event. Finally admitting I couldn't handle it set off a wave of relief along with a rush of feeling utterly stupid. Why had I insisted on putting myself through that? Minute by minute, my life is an endurance test. So unbearably hard. Why had I even contemplated attending an event at the place where he died? Was I punishing myself? Or was I just that desperate for life to return to normal? Looking back on it, I think it's a little of both.

One of my coworker's spouse contacted me in the days after the game—saying she'd missed me. How thoughtful is that? Our employees and their families are kind, goodhearted people. Though most of my interactions with them are of a problem-solving nature, they are the epitome of what companies strive for in seeking employees. Talented people who care about others. I was surprised, first to hear my absence had been noticed, and second that she would take the time to contact me to see how I was faring.

She reminded me that it was okay to not be okay. I know this, of course, but somehow it becomes more acceptable to hear it from someone else. Not sure what that says about me. She said something that resonated with me. "*There is a level of trauma that comes with a sudden loss that is greatly underestimated, especially if you witness it. It is OK to not be OK for as long as it takes*".

I need to remember that. It's okay to not be okay. I so appreciated her taking the time to reach out to me. I have been very fortunate that way. My coworkers and their family members—have really taken care of me. For me, my work has provided the structure I need to get through each day. The one thing that is still *known* in a universe where I don't know much anymore.

# # #

Hindsight: There is no rushing through grief. It's such an obvious truism that I shouldn't even feel the need to type it here, yet that is exactly what I tried to do myself, so maybe you're trying to do it, too. Grief is not a linear process. It's an endless circle. In my case, it's one where I have visited the various steps repeatedly. The shock, the anger, the bargaining. I haven't reached full acceptance yet. We'll see if I ever arrive at that destination. I wish grief could be like a to-do list where I could check off items as I experience them. Then I could throw away the list once I've experienced them all. And then I'm magically happy again.

We need to keep reminding ourselves it is normal to not be okay. It's okay that we're struggling through this endless, sucky process. Even as we embrace our grief, because we have no other choice in the matter, it is okay to acknowledge the terrible hand we've been dealt. We will have unbearable days and if we're lucky, we will eventually have bearable days. That's about all we can hope for at this stage of our journey.

Sometimes we can talk about our loss and sometimes we can't. When I could manage a conversation, I felt a sense of accomplishment. I think it's therapeutic to talk about Dan. About that horrible night that changed everything. But it's also unbelievably hard because it churns everything up again. I'm crying as I type this. I cry as I type text responses to concerned friends. But afterward, I feel as though I accomplished something. I'm not exactly sure what it is yet, but . . . something.

At this stage of grief, I realized it was good practice to set the expectation bar pretty low on what you can accomplish. For a person used to saying yes all the time, it took me a while to learn to be comfortable saying no. You're not a failure because you're no longer strong. After a lifetime of feeling pretty confident. Strong. Self-assured. I've discovered I'm none of those things. At least, I wasn't at this point. Hopefully those strengths will eventually return. At this point, each day is still an endurance test. We need to appreciate small wins.

Getting through work without crying was a big win in the early days. Getting through an evening by myself was even harder. So often, it was a matter of holding it in all day until I could lower the shields and cry it out. Still with no one there to give me a hug. No one to lie and say everything is going to be better someday. But eventually, it will. Maybe not a 'better' we've ever imagined, but a better version of the life we have now. A better we can tolerate. For now, a good night is a walk with my neighbor. A bad night is when she is too tired to go. Or a thunderstorm that forces us to cancel which leaves an extra hour of alone time I'd rather not have.

# # #

13 weeks: Feeling Guilty At thirteen weeks I wonder when I will stop counting weeks. As though at the end of it, there'll be some sort of prize. After 40 weeks, fortunate women receive a baby for their efforts. In twenty-seven more weeks, I can only pray this grief process will have become easier. I'd settle for less hard. Or slightly less painful. Maybe a notch below heartbreaking. I hope by 40 weeks, I will not still be crying every night. By 40 weeks I hope I'm not still approaching the end of the work week with a shiver of dread over the thought of enduring an entire weekend alone. Maybe by 40 weeks, I will have learned to embrace my aloneness. That possibly, I will have found a way to not fear it. To be more accepting of the situation I cannot change. If I can't have Dan back, (and I'm finally starting to believe that is no longer an option), then can I please have acceptance? Can I have a little less pain? Maybe just one day off a week? Could I have a day or two off from crying? It's so exhausting. Or could I maybe experience less doubt? Less fear? Of both the present and the so much bleaker future than I'd ever envisioned?

How about guilt? Can I ever just accept that what happened was God's will? That there was nothing HE or I, or anyone could have done to prevent it? Can you possibly help me let go of my anger and frustration? That the best man I've ever known— the most phenomenal father, the kindest, most generous man I had the privilege of knowing is gone. Far too early. Can I stop being angry that he is gone while so many lesser specimens still walk this earth? That older, less healthy, less generous people who do absolutely nothing for others— are still here? Taking up space. Contributing nothing. Abusing or ignoring their children. While my kindhearted, give-you-the-shirt-off-his-back guy who would help anyone has been taken.

Can anyone help me with that? Because I'm having a great deal of trouble accepting it. Other than that, I'm doing fine. Please God, if you can't grant me any of the above, can you just make this awful time go faster? Can you give me some strength? Can you help me find my way through this? Because the forest is dark and my flashlight batteries feel as though they're fading. I'm growing tired of being strong— of faking being strong. I'm tired of pretending that I'm doing okay. I'm tired, God. Of everything.

# # #

3 months: Weighty Issues I was visiting a coworker in hospice yesterday. Six of us made the journey downtown, knowing her time is very limited. A woman I've known for 19 years. She is 73 and dying of lung cancer. Yes— this has been quite a year for sorrow and disaster. But she is facing death with strength and stoicism (do we have any choice?). She commented on how "skinny" I was. I forced a smile and responded that it was a terrible diet to be on. She shot me an understanding glance and whispered, "I get it". Because she, too, has lost too much weight in her battle with cancer. Unlike my battle with grief where I don't know my outcome, she knows she will not emerge victorious from hers.

While victorious is not an appropriate word for surviving grief, I realized in that moment that I was grateful to be me instead of her. As the others suddenly eyeballed me, I could tell they were surprised at how much weight I have lost, maybe because they see me every day at work. Whereas we hadn't been able to visit our coworker due to the risk of infection, so she hasn't seen me since a few months before Dan died. I'm sure to her, I probably look pretty rough now. It's awkward when someone comments on how 'good' I look. I know the comments are truly well meaning, but I'm caught off guard as to how I should react.

I've lost 25 pounds in a traumatic way; due to horrendous circumstances. It's not something I feel good about. It's not something I feel *anything* about. I'm really rather numb to most things these days. Yet, at some point in the future, I will likely be grateful I'm less heavy. That I'm eating healthier. That I hopefully won't drop dead of a heart attack and devastate my kids' lives any more than they have been destroyed this year. It's a tough way to lose weight. I still need to lose 25 more, so it's not as though I'm wasting away! My goal will be to keep going, but hopefully I will do so in a healthier state of mind.

Grief is very unpredictable these days. In the beginning, it was ever-present. A constant companion. A heavy sweater I could never peel off, even when I was suffocating under it; one I imagined wearing every moment of every day for the rest of my life.

Three months in, grief is still in the forefront. But now, it's become an almost comforting feeling. Like an old friend you can't remember *not* knowing. It is still close to the surface. When you have a decent day; one where you didn't tear up several times, you become hopeful. Maybe it's finally beginning to abate. Maybe I've *finally* turned a corner. Maybe there will start to be more good days than bad. More strong days than helpless. More days where I can smile without feeling pain.

The next day, grief comes at you like a mugger. Springing out of the darkness. A quick punch to the face when you weren't expecting an attack. Dropping you to your knees all over again. And you are filled with doubt over any sense of progress you've made.

Can you make progress in feeling less lonely? What defines *less* lonely? Is it missing your best friend a little less? Is it the ability to laugh occasionally and not feel guilty? Does the ache inside ever subside? The knot in your stomach loosen? Do you reach a point where you just can't cry anymore? If that's the case, I haven't reached it. I've only achieved a few entire days so far. It's hard to imagine I ever will. But I'm trying, Dan. I'm trying really hard to do this without you.

# # #

14 weeks: Friends Something amazing happened this week. A sign, perhaps. On Saturday morning, I was sitting at my computer, crying for the 90th day in a row— when my neighbor texted, out of the blue, inviting me to have coffee on her porch. I could have said no, but I didn't want to. I wiped my eyes, ran upstairs and threw on my clothes. To hide my red eyes, I shoved my sunglasses on and headed over.

On a light-filled, breezy morning I was able to unclench; to settle my churning stomach; to quiet the roar of desperation I feel on most weekends. The voice that tells me I can't go on like this. The voice that says I can't possibly fill all the empty hours. Instead, I sipped coffee and enjoyed conversation with my godsend neighbor who has kept me sane through this gut-wrenching process of moving forward. After coffee, we took a walk for another half hour before going our separate ways.

Just that sliver of time spent with a friend was enough to settle me; to boost my confidence and propel me through another Saturday on my own. On Sunday— another miracle. I'd forced myself to go out; to see a movie by myself and to make a Target run for stuff I didn't really need but the trip would keep me occupied for an additional half hour. On my drive back, a song came on the radio that reminded me of Dan. Since it no longer takes anything to start the tears flowing, i I was instantly crying again. Thirty seconds later, my phone rang. It was my friend, Sue calling to check in with me. I hadn't talked with her since the funeral, but—like a tiny sign from God, she called at that particular moment and I answered, even though I shouldn't talk and drive.

My tears dried up as we caught up for the next hour. And I realized later how much it had meant to chat with her. To laugh. To catch up. I've missed so many of these little moments. These heartwarming conversations. I resolve to try harder. To reach out more to everyone. To not think of myself as an annoyance or an interruption to their day— and instead try to be the good friend they have all been to me.

So, thank you God, for that. Both for the support at a low point in my ongoing series of low points and for the kick in the pants I needed to remind me that I, too must reach out for the help I need. For the friendships I want to nourish. For the forward momentum I need to build. Thanks for that.

# # #

15 weeks: Vacations Tomorrow, I'm heading out on vacation— the first one without Dan. I booked this trip last winter, before he passed away. I am desperate to see the girls. Looking forward to seeing their boyfriends. My brother is coming for a few days and bringing my mother. I am looking forward to seeing everyone. To spending a week together. To getting away from work, despite my need for the structure and the security it provides me. I want so much to just laugh a little bit.

Yet, it's hard not to think about last year's vacation. How much fun we had. How eager Dan was to see the girls. He was always such a larger-than-life presence. Will it feel too quiet without him there? Will I spend the week being sad? Longing for something that can no longer be? Will I feel guilty that he's missing so damn much? If you're watching, Dan— are you happy for us? Resentful that you're not here with us? It never seemed as though we had enough time off together. More often than not, it felt like we *couldn't* get away. The hurricane that cancelled our beach trip last fall. The snowstorm that cancelled our weekend in West Virginia. That would have been the weekend before you died. Instead, we spent that Saturday cleaning the house— because the girls were coming home for Easter the following weekend.

How ironic that we spent the last Saturday of his life cleaning the house for his funeral. All the visitors who would descend on us the week after Easter. Dan was supposed to be on vacation the week after he died. His once-a-year splurge trip to Atlantic City. I was supposed to be heading to Quebec with the high school posse. A forty-year reunion trip. Instead, we cancelled for Dan's funeral. My friends trekked five hundred miles to be here with me instead.

Were vacations just bad luck for us? It was starting to seem that way. I pray this coming week will be better. I pray I will be able to have fun. I need to relax. To unclench. But I wonder. Can I let go enough to enjoy it? Will I waste my family's brief time together on wishing? Wanting? Being sad despite the desperate need to be surrounded by people who make me happy? Or can I embrace this? Enjoy the hell out of it? Be thankful every moment for our beautiful girls? Can I be happy just because we really, really need it? Or will everything be tinged with sadness?

Is it wrong for me to want both? I want to embrace this week. To not think ahead to when I'm driving back home alone again. Sad that it's over. Lonely again. Yet, relieved because another week has passed. Because it counts as progress. Moving forward. The first 'first vacation' over and done. Does that mean next year's vacation will automatically feel better? Or am I wasting an opportunity? To embrace the new situation. Be thankful for being together after a catastrophic change. Will I look at our group picture this time and wonder whether our group will all still be here next year? Because when I look at last year's beach picture, I'm still stunned into silence. That the largest personality in the frame is no longer here. Please, let us get through this week, happier and stronger.

# # #

16 weeks: I dreamed of Dan last week. The fourth night of our vacation, he visited me in a dream. It was so real, I shook myself awake so I could talk with him. I sat up in bed, looking for him. But he wasn't there. Though he looked tired, he smiled at me. But it was a wistful smile. Maybe even regretful? Hell, I'm probably reading too much into it. Dan handed me a key. It was bright and shiny, an old fashioned, Victorian sort— like it fit an ancient lock. I don't know what door it was for, nor what my mind was hoping he was telling me.

I felt his presence, too. The night we all gathered at the winery to play trivia, as we did last year. All of us pretending not to notice Dan wasn't there. Literally the first question was about baseball. The girls shot me a worried look like 'is she going to be okay'? Then later, Barry Manilow came on. *Copa Cabana*— one of his favorites— and by then Miranda was dancing at the table. We were all smiling. Joking. The wine was flowing. And the night was very fun.

Last week was fun. And sad. And different from any vacation before it. How could it not be after 36 years together? In reflecting on the week now that I'm back home, I feel as though I experienced a breakthrough of sorts. Dan, I missed you so much. The first vacation without you. The first vacation without your big personality, your jovial good nature, your spare-no-expense way of doing whatever it takes to ensure everyone feels welcome and has a good time. Yet, despite the gaping hole you've left in our lives, we carried on.

We had a wonderful vacation, though tinged with sadness. I experienced six days with no crying, though I admit the tears all found their way back to me on the long drive home yesterday. And believe me, I've been working overtime on them today. But I must admit I enjoyed the temporary reprieve. I enjoyed laughing. I spent quiet, insightful time walking each morning with my brother. Knots I hadn't known were residing in my stomach began to slowly unwind as I rocked on the porch with my 85-year-old mother.

It was so good; so comforting to be around family for an entire week. It was so great to see the girls with their boys. To see how happy they are together. It drove home the reality of how hard this situation has been without Dan here to make it better. Without the girls here. With what's left of my family living 500 miles away. Managing by myself for each of the hundred days he's been gone.

Dan's death has been a nightmare I would never wish upon the worst enemy. But for that single week of vacation from grief, I felt surrounded by family. By our loving daughters and their kind-hearted and generous boyfriends. By my frail, yet still feisty mother. By a brother who also has experienced loss by way of divorce. It was so comforting to not feel alone for seven glorious days. It's not as though I wish our vacation couldn't end, but the family part— I wish I could have more of that. Together, I feel we would be so much stronger as a whole instead of the individual components we are now. Living far apart.

Yet, for now . . . living in this awful black tunnel, I am alone. I will bear it, because I know Dan wouldn't want me to give up. I can't fail our daughters who have already borne too much. But God it is so hard without him. As I sit here alone again, waiting for it to be late enough to fall into bed, I pray I will sleep so I can get up and go to work tomorrow.

# # #

Hindsight: The boyfriends. These beautiful, thoughtful, wonderful boys. Two young gentlemen who walked into the fire. Likely with terror in their hearts. Those awful early days, my daughters' boyfriends' faces told the real story. They'd never had to face the death of someone close. Someone they knew. And this death would be a big one. A potential relationship game-changer. A possible deal breaker, based on the unknown future emotional fallout.

They weren't facing one of the classic first relationship hurdles with the *comparatively easy* death of a distant grandparent who had lived a long, comfortable life and passed quietly in their sleep. These boys had to take on a Big Loss. A deeply sad, life-altering, traumatizing loss. Of a too young, larger-than-life, seriously involved Dad with a capital D. A loss that would unquestionably change their partner. A shockwave that would reverberate through their relationships going forward.

These boys were about to be bitch-slapped with grief. Yet, with fear in their hearts, they continued walking forward into the all-encompassing gray mist. In the early days, they drove hours back and forth to wedge in enough work so they wouldn't be fired from corporate jobs that didn't understand the need for time off for "their girlfriend's dad". Who was that person to them? *You're not even married yet* was the likely corporate response. Yet, they still did it. Unwilling to leave our daughters' sides that first week. Unable to prevent them from drowning in grief, but resolute that they would battle to keep the girls' heads above the thrashing waves.

Today I am remembering and reflecting on their bravery. When they insisted they needed to help me with the funeral planning. Boyfriend

1 drawing the short straw of driving me to the funeral home to identify Dan's body before cremation because he didn't want either of the girls having to go. Boyfriend 2 sitting through the long, sad, surreal planning of Dan's funeral service. And that was merely the start of their tough days to come. They had to learn to recognize and comfort grief that could potentially be a game changer to their relationships.

Miranda's boyfriend requested a job transfer so he could move back to Pitt to be closer to her in the early days after Dan's death. He had only moved to DC eight months earlier. Yet, he moved all of his stuff back to Pitt just to be there for her. While it was life changing for Miranda to not be alone in the endless gray months after her father died; it was life altering for me too. To know my youngest, who was six hours away from me, was no longer alone as she learned to navigate the anguishing reality of our new lives. It provided such comfort to know he would be there with her.

When I look back, I think about all the people who swallowed their fear; who suited up for battle and just showed up. Entering a house consumed with grief and tears and sadness. They had to have dreaded it. Had to know it would be gut-wrenching and god awful. Yet, they did it anyway. They showed up. They hugged and cried and prayed and coffee-caked us. They organized meal trains. They delivered pizza on day two and three to feed the throng of family that began showing up. After the first week, when you're running on adrenaline and no sleep and worse— when everyone goes home and back to their lives, the door closes and your 'new life' awaits you. These battle-scarred warriors are the ones who keep showing up. They keep you busy.

They invited me to their homes. Likely, they were dreading it. What will she be like? Will she cry? Will it be depressing? When it would be so easy to *sort of* forget. Your true friends will keep after you. They will persist in inviting you into their lives. They will invite you into their 'normal' because they know you don't have that anymore.

My brave friends, these *saints* were like, 'what are you doing this weekend? Do you have plans? We'd love you to come to dinner. Come with us to our son's ballgame. Meet me Saturday morning at the gym and then we can get breakfast. Hop on the train and come for a girls' weekend' and so on. These people are your friends. The true, fearless friends who just dive in, not knowing how deep the water is. They know it will probably be awkward. Uncomfortable. They knew they might be hit by unexpected grief. They suspected they would be exhausted and relieved once the evening was over. Once I was gone. Yet, they did it anyway. That's love.

My neighbor has literally walked hundreds of miles with me. Every night, for both exercise and to keep me sane. Hundreds of miles slogged together. Walking and talking and praying and the occasional shared laugh. Because no matter how bleak your life can get; there are still things to laugh about. These people are your gifts. Embrace them as such. I pray I can be the same steady presence to them when the time comes that they ever need me as I have needed them.

# # #

17 weeks: Reality Check This week I fainted. Out of the blue. No warning. I'd finally summoned the courage to venture out on my own, to a Meetup event with two women who were exceptionally nice. A summer theatre Shakespeare production Dan would have hated. But I, being desperately lonely, was enthusiastic, and terribly nervous—a new place to find. New people to introduce myself to. Not my better skills on display.

I found the place- it's beautiful and definitely worth a trip back during the day when the house and grounds will be open. But for that night, it was just a pretty place to have a picnic on the lawn with two kind strangers I could pretend were friends I knew well. They welcomed me with open arms. We had a picnic on the lawn before heading into the garden to watch the play. It was a warm night, but not stifling. There was a breeze. Yet, midway through the first act, I started to feel strange. My stomach, which had been bothering me all day (likely over the dread of a new adventure that night) began to hurt again. I started sweating, and before I knew what hit me, I was feeling as though I might pass out.

I fought it, the overwhelming dread of being in a strange place with sweat pouring down my forehead, sitting next a near stranger; trying desperately not to faint—and to attempt looking 'normal' while it was happening. When the woman next to me nudged me to ask if I was okay, I jarred back to consciousness. I was too sick to feel shame, but I knew it had happened. I'd fainted in front of strangers enjoying a Shakespeare comedy under the night sky. With rubbery legs, I waited for the awful, sick sensation to pass—at least enough for me to unsubtly climb down the steps at the tiny venue and take refuge in the bathroom. When I felt well enough to move, I made my apologies to the two women I'd only just met, and I slunk away.

On the drive home—missing half the play I'd been enjoying; I was drenched with sweat and relief. That it hadn't been worse. That I hadn't embarrassed myself further. My attempt at trying something new had failed. Worse, it had raised a red flag of fear that had been simmering under the surface for months. I am alone. I have no one to help me. If something like this occurred on a regular basis—what would I do? It makes me fearful of trying new things—running exactly counter to what I feel I SHOULD be doing. I need to get out there. I need to make friends. I need to DO things to get out of this eerily still mausoleum.

Yet, I tried it—and failed. I could have fallen. Hit my head. Among strangers. How do I learn to be alone confidently? I hate being fearful—it's never been who I am. Or maybe, I've always been that way? And Dan masked it for me?

On the plus side, I heard from the Meetup woman, not once, but twice that night after I left. She was so kind. It made me wish we really were friends. She checked up on me. She offered to drop off meds for stomach flu. It was so sweet of her. I am grateful to have met her. On the minus side, I'd had plans to go to another Meetup dinner the next night with a different group, but I cancelled. I was still too frazzled—I was too insecure to handle the thought of something else happening to me.

But I will try again this coming week. A dinner next Tuesday night for widows. At least I'll know they're members of the same suck ass club I've joined. And if I can meet someone else who has made it through this—maybe I'll feel better? Maybe I'll learn that the magic number is a year? Or two? Or just get a clue about—any of it. I need to learn something about what I'm facing for the rest of my life. About how to manage the aloneness. About how to not fear the risks involved in this new, unchosen life. About how they endured it. And how I will have to learn to endure it, too. So, wish me luck in meeting with a group of women who are hopefully not as pathetic as me right now.

The other thing I worry about is what will this do to the girls? On one hand, I feel I need to better hide my grief from them—get a handle on it so they don't worry about me. On the flip side, this is so frigging awful. It's the worst thing I've ever endured. So, how the hell do I hide something this big from them? Plus, I need to let it out. I need to lean on them occasionally. Dan would be so proud of them. They are here for me. Chelsea especially has come home so often. I know it's such a burden on her. But God—I miss her when she leaves. While she's here, we can almost forget for a minute or two WHY she's actually visiting. For an hour or two, it will feel normal. Like—maybe Dan is at a baseball game and we're strolling through Target. Waiting for him to come home so we can all head out for Mexican food. But then we remember.

We get a table for two instead of three. And try not to look at each other as we're both thinking the same thing. He's not here. He's not coming back. And we have to talk about it. Acknowledge how much we miss him. She's hurting so much, too. As is Miranda. But, now on top of their own grief, they have the burden of me to worry about. I pray I will regain some of my strength sooner rather than later. I hate feeling weak. I hate feeling vulnerable. I hate that our girls are worried about me—instead of the other way around. It's not supposed to work this way. We were supposed to be here to take care of them. Protect them. Guide them. And now—I'm just a floundering, useless mess. I don't want to cause them worry. Yet, I am unable to shore myself up enough to hide the fact that I'm a basket case most days.

# # #

Hindsight: In fairness to myself, I was getting incrementally better at this point. But, like weight loss, it's hard to notice day to day that you're improving. It's easy to keep beating yourself up and believing you're a failure. You think life is pretty hopeless and you'll never make it on your own. Until you begin taking baby steps. Maybe the attempt will go well. Maybe it won't. But the bottom line is that you made *the attempt*. Like weight loss, we have successes, and we have days when we eat a pint of ice cream.

The day you can finally give yourself credit for your attempts to feel better will feel similar to the day you are courageous enough to step on the scale and discover you're five pounds lighter. Grief does get better, eventually. But this stage was such a raw, vulnerable time for me. I don't really have any words of wisdom, except that you can only tackle it one day at a time. Sometimes, it felt like I was back in early days again, where time was measured in minutes. And then hours. Just know that you will get through it because you have to.

Hindsight 2: MeetUp groups: During this time, I checked out several Meetup groups (remember this was pre-pandemic) that were potentially fun ways to meet people who like the same things you do. There are book and movie clubs; brunch clubs; hiking; widows dinner groups; camping and travel, etc. for people who want to attend events but would rather not go alone. If I hadn't been at such a fragile low point, I think I would have jumped into far more events than I actually summoned the courage to attend. I assume Meetup groups will begin thriving again as we finally move beyond the pandemic.

I did a lot of reading during this time – when my brain was able to focus for more than fifteen minutes. I have a list of books that were of varying levels of usefulness for me. There are also several Facebook groups for widows I began to seek out (list at the end). Again, varying levels of usefulness, but there was always someone on there who was going through what I was. That alone provided comfort to me. I was not alone in my aloneness.

# # #

4 months: Anger and Frustration I've discovered I don't like flowers anymore. This week, a friend from grade school was celebrating her birthday. As I wrote out her card, I realized she hadn't heard the news. She lives 300 miles away. Both of us with busy lives; me with a sudden and traumatic grief. It can do a number on your friendships. So, as I awkwardly pondered how to tell her, I was both crying and chuckling as I wrote out her card. Happy birthday!! Hope all is well. Me? Not so much. My note to her was as surreal as you could imagine. I can only imagine being on the receiving end of a card like that.

Her receipt prompted a phone call from her, which I ended up missing because I was out on a therapy walk with my neighbor. I was sort of glad to miss the call, truthfully. I'm not sure why this is, exactly, but talking about Dan's death is usually far harder than writing about it. Don't get me wrong. Writing about it is seriously hard, too. But most of the time I find I can text with someone easier than I can talk.

Anyway, her phone call back to me was the start of a text string conversation. And several follow-ups from her. Friendships are a strange and wonderful thing I think we tend to take for granted. Sometimes it is too easy to forget the bonds that once tied us. For some friendships, the bonds only seem to strengthen instead of fraying. Over distance, space and time, they are still there, gently tugging, even during the most hectic times of our lives; they tether us to the past. Like a balloon tied to our wrist, just bouncing along with us.

So the worst birthday card in history led to the phone call which led to the text messages. Which led to cards from both her sister and brother, a flashback to our elementary school days. This week, gifts started arriving. First, a gorgeous arrangement of flowers. Next, a lovely package of lotions and stress relieving treats. So incredibly thoughtful. A quiet reminder that someone out there is thinking of me as I slog through another day without Dan.

After a tough day at work, I arrived home to find the lovely arrangement of roses and summer daisies on the porch. Which leads me to the realization that my relationship with flowers has radically changed. After 36 years of receiving them whimsically, I had grown to love their presence in the house. If Dan didn't bring them home on his way home after work, I'd usually buy them at the grocery store to match my mood— or the season or the tablecloth.

But now, after receiving nearly 50 arrangements for his funeral, I no longer smile when I receive them. I'm appreciative of the sentiment behind them, of course. And I can admire their beauty, but I no longer seek them out. Maybe that will change someday. I sort of hope so. I'd hate to think I've lost one of life's simpler pleasures. Flowers used to make me smile.

This week has been some sort of turning point. Not that I feel any better, but I'm starting to feel tired and perhaps a little frustrated. It's likely my own fault. In trying to seize control of the very few things I can control, I realize I'm tired of hearing the word no. I finally— like five years too late, went for a physical; I fasted; I waited an hour; I discussed my life with the clinically dispassionate doc-in-a-box physician. Again, my fault for not finding a primary care physician. Another item added to my to-do list. I did all the blood work so I could turn over a new leaf. Start taking care of myself. Find out my numbers. Yada, yada, yada. And Tuesday night, over three weeks after my appointment— the doc-in-a-box finally calls me to fess up that they lost my blood sample 'in transit'. Could I please come in to do it all over again?? What does that mean? Did it fall off the truck? Did the driver drop it? Smash the tubes in a fit of rage? Was it sold on the dark web? What about my urine? Is that lost too? Or did it just sit in a back room at your facility and petrify while you all gabbed about Game of Thrones?

Should I now have MORE faith in your ability to do it right the next time?? And of course— I'm sure I won't be billed for this second round of tests! Because you clearly have your act together. I'm sure it won't take 17 phone calls and my bill going to collections for your tiny little error of my blood being 'lost in transit'. I only get one free physical a year; or in my case—the last 5 years. And now I know even less information than I knew before the appointment. Except—shame on me for not finding a real doctor. Yeah, it's been that kind of week.

Sometimes it's just a suggestion that manages to set me off. From a professional— whose advice I'm actually seeking, mind you. Maybe do this instead of that— as I try to rebuild my life. As I make decisions to try to clean up my finances, so the girls have an easier time down the road. As I talk to the experts whose help I am seeking, is it wise to want to disregard some of what they advise?

This week was a lawyer; an accountant and my beloved friend who is taking care of my life insurance claim. Yes— Big Insurance Company, it's now been four months since I filed Dan's life claim.

How much more investigating can you do? He's still dead. I didn't kill him. And he very publicly didn't kill himself. What more can you possibly need to know? I realize you didn't break even on this one. I'm sorry Dan died before you'd extracted enough premium.

But the stress you're causing me, on top of the biggest loss I pray I will ever endure, has likely shortened my own life. Not that I care so much, but my daughters probably do. They've been through enough for now. So, could you just pay the fucking claim already? Maybe fire your actuary? Or tighten up your risk factors going forward? In the meantime, you're really stressing me out.

For four months I've wondered— can I pay all the bills on one salary now? Will it be manageable? Or crazy hard? Can I make a dent in my mortgage with the insurance proceeds? So, if I lose my job or in this case, have a stress-induced stroke— I won't be homeless? Could you just cough it up already, Big Insurance Bully? It's not as though I'm planning a trip around the world with the money. Just a trip to the grocery store. Can I afford a full pound of cherries? They're heading out of season, so it would be nice to splurge a little. How about Trader Joe's? Can I afford to shop there once a month?

I find it soothing to walk around Trader Joe's. I don't know why. Even though I don't cook much, can I afford to buy a couple Trader Joe's frozen dinners? Could you let me know soon, Insurance Bully who can afford to pay me but chooses not to? Wish your check was here! Sincerely, your increasingly desperate client.

# # #

Hindsight: Stress. At some point in this process, you will be trying to do too much. Trying to cover too many bases at once. You will be angry and frustrated. And you will be completely overwhelmed like

I was. I needed to take my own advice and just breathe. Slow down. Do a few less tasks from my list. The list will still be there tomorrow. And the next day. But let's face it. We can be our own worst enemies. Try not to do that to yourself. Take it from me. It really doesn't help.

# # #

5 months: Reality Check I thought I was starting to get the hang of this. The alone thing. The realization that Dan isn't coming back. That it's not just a bad dream. I know that because I still don't sleep through the night most nights. I see his eyes. Staring at me, with the most bewildered, and now that I look back— frightened expression I'd ever seen. 36 years of glances from him, and I'd never seen that one. I couldn't translate it. Now that it's seared into my memory, I wonder if I'll ever forget. If I'll ever stop seeing it. It's the vision I have before I fall asleep. I wonder if I'll ever stop wondering whether he knew how bad it was. How it would end. How terrified he must have been. Because I seriously didn't know. I didn't know when he walked away that last time it would BE the last time. Even as a shiver of worry clenched my stomach, I tried to shrug it off. That it was me worrying over nothing. That I was 'over-reacting' as he'd usually claim. Instead, it was my greatest fear being realized. With no opportunity to fight it.

No second chance to make it better. To change the course. No chance for me to bully him into a better diet. For him to promise to try harder. Eat better. Lose weight. No chance for a 'minor' heart attack to scare him straight. It just ended. In one single, final heartbeat, his life ended. And mine ended too. The happiness part. The gratefulness that we were so lucky part. Now, I'm just here. Existing. Happy for the few days every month when I see the girls. Grateful I have work to fill my days. The rest of the time is mostly nothingness. Anxiety about the future. Fear of how long I'll be here alone.

I thought I was making progress. Somewhere in the last month I stopped crying every day. I thought it was because I'd accepted it. Given up. My brain knows Dan is gone. And crying certainly won't bring him back. Logic dictates I have to stop sometime, right? But as I left the movie theater tonight, tears started rolling down my face. I was crossing the parking lot, and they just started. Before I could get the car door open, I was sobbing. All the way home, to our darkened, empty house. Where I spend evenings pacing the rooms. Watching TV. Staring at his empty chair. Reading to fill my restless mind with something to calm it. Thinking of all the time we've missed. All the things I haven't been able to tell him.

I started to write the important things down on a pad— as though he'd be returning sometime. As though he's just been . . . missing these last five months. As though I'll get the chance to catch him up— and I don't want to forget anything. And then I realize this is my life now. My new, shattered, lonely life. Endless hours to fill. With things that don't matter. Days to count off. Weeks and months and years to measure. Until the pain goes away. Or dulls. Or just eases a tiny bit.

I experience rational moments of trying to find reasons I should be grateful instead of bitter. To remind myself I need to stay strong for the girls, while knowing it's just an act. I have moments when I try to analyze what this is all supposed to mean. What is the takeaway? Because so far it has been a bottomless pit of grief. It has been enough tears to fill a small pond. It has been enough Kleenex for me to wish I'd bought their stock years ago. And an endless, lonely ache that I fear will never leave me. I try to tell myself tomorrow will be better. But then I remember— tomorrow will be just like today. Only it will be 5 months and one day without him. How can tomorrow be better? Realistically, all I can hope for is less bad. I can hope the pain will be less bad. The missing Dan ache will lessen. The loneliness will become less pronounced. The by-myself ness will feel less strange.

I overhear women and their jokey commiserating about husbands working late; about them leaving laundry on the floor. About controlling the television remote and I just cringe. I see the couples still together who don't even like each other. Who barely *tolerate* each other- And I want to scream. My father always loved to boast that nice guys finish last. And he was the ultimate bastard, so he truly knew what he was talking about. I always rebelled against that notion. Because, of all people, Dan was the nicest man I'd ever met. There wasn't an unkind bone in his body. So, it leaves me asking why. Why did my bastard father live to see 78? He wouldn't cross the room to help anyone. Why do so many awful, horrible people live so long?

Why did God do this to us? To US? When he could have broken up couples who would likely feel some sense of relief. Who maybe would have rejoiced? When I would have gratefully, happily, willingly spent the next thirty years with you. My grief counselor recommended the book "When Bad Things Happen to Good People".

It helped me view death in a slightly different perspective. And it tried to portray God in a gentler light. But, at the end of the day, I can't shake the feeling that God failed my husband. Maybe he's not punishing me. Punishing our girls. But it still feels that way. In a world so filled with hate and injustice, Dan's death feels like a victory for the bastards of this world. The bullies. The narrow-minded people who either rejoice in or have become immune to the daily cruelty that has become our norm. Or maybe I just read this book too soon. Maybe I'm not ready yet. I'm not sure I'll attempt reading it again.

While I wrestle with my anger with God, I'm not ashamed to admit to being two-faced. I still pray fiercely to Him that there really is a heaven. And that Dan is there. And that it's been worth it. That he's happy. At peace. Because no one on this earth deserves it more than Dan, and I would be shattered to know I had to give him up for anything less than perfection. Utopia.

It better be amazing, Dan. You talked about it often enough. That we'd see each other again. On the 'other side'. I have to admit I'm questioning my belief right now. But Dan never did. And I've never not believed in him—therefore, I will continue to believe in heaven. So you'd better be waiting when I finally get there. Because I'll be looking for you. And if it's not bliss, and you're not ecstatic to be there, I'm going to be seriously pissed off.

# # #

Hindsight: Counseling. Meeting with a grief counselor can be very beneficial. If you haven't considered it, don't rule it out. I met with a lovely woman who'd been trained in trauma counseling. In seeking her out, I did some research into trauma because I had been experiencing PTSD – in the form of the horrible, crippling flashbacks of Dan's last night. Even if you don't feel it will be helpful, there is always something you can gain from speaking with a professional. And – if you have benefits at work, you probably have an EAP (employee assistance) program. This is how I met with my counselor. The first three visits were free because of my EAP at work.

These benefits are often under-mentioned to employees, only because we worry more about the 'big' benefits like health insurance, etc. But you should look into the presence of an EAP because you can tap into those free visits as a "try before you buy". If you really click with the counselor, then you can pay for follow up visits using your health insurance. If you don't get on with the counselor, you can try someone else and you haven't spent your own money yet. Seriously consider talking with someone.

# # #

5.5 months: Keep busy. That's what everyone says. Stay as *busy* as possible. As though I'm outrunning a pack of hungry wolves. Like if I slow down for a minute, I'll be knocked down and ravaged by the pack. I don't know if I have the stamina for *keeping busy* much longer. My friend told me that last night, his eyes so utterly *knowing* as he stares through my facade. R's beautiful wife, the center of his universe, passed away two years ago. Not one year— but *two*. He still keeps busy to the extreme. He was always a generous, giving man.

And now he's turbo charged generosity with the gift of his time. I'm left to wonder. At 5.5 months in, do I have that kind of endurance? *Keep busy*. As though there might be a way to outrun the loneliness that has settled around me like dense fog.

Unfortunately, loneliness is here for the long haul. My constant companion as I go to bed each night (notice I didn't say 'sleep') and she's waiting for me when I wake each morning— typically, two hours too early. Each day fresh with the painful realization Dan is still gone. Some days, I almost forget. I experience the briefest flash of hope— that somehow life will start getting better again. Like I've only amputated a leg—and it should be healing by now. Like— maybe I'll be walking again soon. And then I remember what's happened. The permanence of it. That it's not a leg. It's a heart. They were joined, and now his is gone. And I'm stuck trying to breathe with only half. But my half doesn't really know how to work without Dan's. Maybe that's why I'm only half alive now.

Dan would have been so excited last weekend. Labor Day, when we believe we're drifting into fall, but the heat won't actually break for another month. UVA won their first football game last weekend. Did he know? Was he watching? It would be the ultimate irony if Virginia finally has a winning season this year. After Dan religiously followed them for so many painful, losing years.

Dan's friend M who attended every game with him said they were *supposed* to win, so it's not really a sign. I wanted to ask him what it was like to now be attending games without Dan, but I was afraid to go there. I think he was, too. He was with us the night Dan died. He went to the hospital with us. Retrieved his car from the ballfield late that night. I know Dan's death it has affected him. How could it not? He really misses you, Dan. We always teased you about your bromance, but you truly were the best of friends.

M insisted on paying for dinner last night. He explained that Dan had paid for so many outings during the year when M had been out of work. I'm not sure if I knew that, but it sounded so much like Dan. To nudge his friend into going out. Dan had known firsthand the burden of depression that can come when you're out of work too long. So, he would call his friend and nudge him to go to a game because Dan knew it would lift his spirits. All those Friday night high school football games.

Dan used to build a chart in Excel—of all the games they needed to attend. It was very strategic. All the local games; which school was hosting; numerous discussions with his friend to rank importance of team matchups to determine which games were vital to attend. Plotting strategy on parking and traffic and seats. And so much effort into where they'd go afterwards. God, they had so much fun. And at so little cost.

Our retirement would have been so fun for Dan. Baseball, football, high school, college, minor league. He didn't care what time of year it was; what sport was in season. Only that he was outside in the sun or in the cool night breeze. He had a hotdog and a beer and he was rejoicing in life. He'd often talked about a part-time job at a stadium so he could make a little money and see all the games for free.

How many times did he send me and the girls a picture of the sun setting over the ballpark? Dan truly was a person who enjoyed every minute of every experience. Maybe it was right that he died in the stadium he loved so much. Where he'd spent so much time. Sometimes I wonder if he's still hanging out there . . . but I can't make myself go back. Maybe in a couple years I could handle it. Maybe I would feel his presence. Maybe it would make me feel better. But, for now, I just can't do it. I can barely handle driving past it.

As much as I miss him, I'm sure his friend had it worse last Saturday— the first college game without Dan sitting beside him in the stands. Without his goofy jokes. Without Dan's haggling ability, he likely paid full price to their favorite scalper for his ticket. Baseball season is nearly over. The Sox had a nice run, but they're back to choking now, as usual. The local minor league baseball season is over. I'm not sure how well they did. I couldn't bear to read about it.

I'm sad Dan missed all those games. The season hadn't even started when he left us. He would attend about thirty of those minor league games each season, especially on Friday nights because it was free T-shirt night. I wonder if the T-shirt girl at the baseball stadium missed him this year. Over all these years, she'd gotten to know him— the only 3x shirt she hands out. She'd gotten to the point where she'd set it aside for him every Friday night because he'd never miss one of those free T-shirt games.

Was she curious when he stopped showing up? Has she been setting aside a shirt for him all season? Wondering whether maybe he'd moved away? Dying likely never occurred to her. Dan was too young for that.

At least he got to attend all the early college baseball games, freezing his ass off at the start of the season in February, sitting there with fifty other people—probably parents out there watching their kids. And Dan—rejoicing as the weather slowly warmed. Eager for all the games to come.

In a twist on the bizarre universe we now live in, Chelsea was contacted by a girl, who, along with her mother, tried to resuscitate Dan that night. The rivalry game is always a sell-out and packed with Virginia alumni. The girl said her mom, a nurse, fought valiantly to save Dan— but the stadium didn't have any defibrillators. A stadium seating over 9,000 people and literally no way to help someone having a heart attack? How is that possible? Instead, the stadium sent us flowers for the funeral. If my humble husband hadn't died that night, I'm sure he would have been deeply flattered by the attention from a place he loved so much. Instead of installing defibrillators, buying flowers every so often is probably the cheaper way to go. And it *was* a lovely arrangement.

Chelsea ended up researching the law and discovered in Virginia, defibrillators are only legally required in schools and hospitals. Seriously? Hospitals—where there are already actual doctors who could help you. What about everywhere else? How can that sort of irresponsibility continue? Apparently, the Virginia mom was so angry, she contacted the stadium manager in the weeks after Dan died. Despite their stall tactics, she refused to be shut down. Likely suffering her own trauma from that night, she persisted in overcoming the stadium's indifference to my husband's unnecessary death.

Supposedly, the ballpark has finally installed two defibrillators. I will probably never be able to return there to confirm this. If true, that number is still far too few for a venue that size, but maybe going forward, it will prevent someone else's dad from dying needlessly. I am forever grateful to the UVA mom who tried to save Dan, as no one in the stadium seemed able to do much until the mom and daughter called 911. I'm grateful Dan did not die alone. I also admire Chelsea's tenacity in researching the reasons why a lifesaving device is treated so flippantly by our state. Maybe someday my strength will return and I too, can try to do something about it.

For now, it's exhausting getting through each day. Trying to keep my grief in check while I'm at work. Trying to keep depression at bay. Trying to stay strong for the girls and for me, always with the hope we will see it through this nightmare to the other side. Still intact. Still together. Forever changed by our loss, but hopefully able to be happy again. It will be a hollow sort of happy, but I pray for it nonetheless. We'll never regain the perfect, unique happy we all had together, but at this point I'll be grateful for whatever the three of us can extract from the ashes.

Dan would have been so happy this season. This year Pitt football is playing UVA in Charlottesville on the Friday night before a wedding we would've all attended together. What a fun weekend that would've been! The girls both here for their friend's wedding. Maybe we would've all gone to the game together. Miranda's boyfriend is coming in for the wedding, so they will likely be attending the game. I'm sure Dan's game buddy will be there too. Chelsea will be busy with wedding stuff for her best friend. I'm not sure if they'll want me to go, too. But big crowds aren't fun for me and now I've become hyper aware of always being the third wheel. I don't want to be a clinging leech on the girls that weekend. It's their school. Their friends. And me.

# # #

Almost 6 months: Hopes and Regrets Clouds of grief seem to have stalled over my head like the remnants of the hurricane that passed through last week. My first hurricane without Dan. Luckily, it made a last-minute turn south. So, as far as firsts go, it wasn't nearly as bad as it could've been. The patio furniture was heavier than I remembered as I tried to flip it over and tie it down. The thought of being alone in howling winds and torrential rain wasn't as bad as imagining being without power for a week. It's still hot and humid, despite it being September. The thought of not sleeping AND sweltering was pretty off-putting. Other firsts since Dan's been gone? I have killed a hornet; a spider; and a gross, multi legged bug in the bathroom sink whose origin I really don't want to contemplate.

I've dealt with ants in the house not once, but twice, thanks to the insane amount of rain we've received this summer. If we get another mouse like that one ten years ago— I might just put the house up for sale.

Despite my grief, or maybe in defiance of it, I bought six fall mums of various sizes and colors. Dan likely would have described my haul as "a shitload", followed closely by "how much did those cost?" But I'm still his girl, always seeking a bargain, so he'd be happy to know they were relatively cheap. I'm decorating a tiny bit, only because fall is my favorite season. But unlike my usual— going crazy with gourds, pumpkins, autumn leaves scattered on every surface, I'm doing a fall tablecloth with a few gourds from Trader Joe's and the pumpkins Chelsea bought me. I think it will cheer me up a little. At the very least, it will acknowledge the changing seasons. Dan has missed a rainy spring, a humid, rainy summer and now, a rainy, hurricane-y fall.

UVA has now won two games. After more than a decade of Dan suffering through loss after loss, it would really be a punch in the face if they finally had a winning season. But, then again, Dan would've been giddy with these wins, so who am I to talk? Maybe he's the reason they're winning. The Patriots won last weekend. I can't watch the games (not that I watched many to begin with) but I'll keep track of the scores for him. Wouldn't it be surprising if every one of Dan's teams had a great year this year? I guess I'd have to look at that as an honor to him. It will still feel like a gut punch to me. The ultimate insult. But if it looks like it's going to happen, I should probably bet heavy, knowing Dan will come through for us.

Another big event this week— I paid off the girls' student loans. It's ironic that something we'd always vowed to take care of before retiring didn't actually provide much pleasure. After all, Dan wasn't here to take pride in our job well done. I guess I don't feel happy because it really *wasn't* a job well done. Dan dying was the sole reason I was able to pay their loans off early. I can assure you we all would've been ecstatic to struggle for several more years to pay them down if it meant Dan could still be here. But since I can't have that, I'd like the girls to have that weight of debt off them. Miranda's loan payment was nearly $ 700 per month. How does anyone save for their future with loans like that to repay? Grad school loans are particularly painful. The financial industry really puts the screws to young people. Grad school loans are not federally subsidized. So, banks and lenders take advantage of kids trying to pursue a graduate degree. With interest rates hovering around 3% for the last ten years, why was Miranda paying 6-8% for her grad school loans? Answer: because they can get away with it. They reap an assload of profit off the backs of our kids. And saddle them with insurmountable debt when they're just starting out. Okay – I'm climbing down off my soapbox,

I've talked with two financial planners now, and each suggested different ways of making sure I can continue paying all the bills. One suggested I should pay the loans off over time. But, at the end of the day, I look at the life insurance money as tainted. It was money I always prayed I would never receive. I'd hoped we would have just run out the term of the insurance. Dan would've only been 74. Instead, I got the money far too early. It's been bothering me to see that money sitting in a money market fund while I waited for someone to advise me what to do with it. When all along, I KNOW what I want to do.

I've counseled the girls to take the huge monthly loan payment they were making and stick it into a savings account—to save for something important. Or an investment account so they can see it grow. I remind them gently that it's important to not just fritter it away every month. They need to do something important with their savings. Something that would make Dan proud. Even though we all know he was always proud of them no matter what. He always said his two greatest accomplishments were our marriage and those perfect girls. I'd have to agree with him on that.

I plan to guilt them occasionally, so they keep him in the back of their minds when they go to the mall and are tempted to buy stupid stuff. As for me, I think I'm going to err on the side of being conservative with the rest of it. Instead of investing in this overripe market, I'm going to pay off the home equity line. It's a sure thing. It will help me monthly by eliminating that payment and thanks to our 'tax cut' I can't write off the interest anymore. Paying it off will save me $4500 annually in interest. If I invested it and lost even a dime, I would feel so much regret because I still view it as that money equaling his life.

I don't have the stomach for risking that money when it was a death blow to receive it. I've also realized that if this had been the other way around, Dan would've been in much worse shape financially. Though it's belated, I apologize for that. Unlike him, I have hardly any life insurance through my work. Which would have left Dan with half as much as he left me. I keep wondering how he would be handling this. The difficult choices he would've been forced to make because I hadn't carried enough life insurance on me. The policies we bought last year were meant to be left to grandchildren in twenty years. WE weren't supposed to need them. Eighteen months later, here I am, alone. And very much needing them!

What if it had been Dan? He would've had some very hard decisions to make. With less money to make them. I'm sorry about that. I've always considered us to be decent financial planners, but boy, did we blow that call. Also unlike him, he would have only received maybe a week of my pro-rated vacation pay after my death. Dan's state benefits gave me about six weeks that he'd stockpiled in anticipation of our retirement. Of course, it took them nearly three months before they finally paid it out. Dan also left me with a tiny pension—not what it would have been at retirement of course, but we'd planned to use that to cover retirement health insurance. Now, it's paying two thirds of the monthly premium of my survivor health insurance I had to purchase. It's wicked expensive. The trade-off is that I can keep it until I become Medicare eligible.

Normally, I would have just jumped on my health insurance at work, but with our life plans blown to smithereens, I'm no longer certain how long I'll remain working here. I'm the only one left. The girls are far flung, at least for the next few years. And our extended families are five hundred miles away. Who knows how long I'll last down here by myself? Since I have eleven years until Medicare, I ended up choosing to overpay for Dan's survivor health insurance so I can keep my options open. If I move and a new job doesn't have health insurance . . . or if I have trouble landing a job— because let's face it, age discrimination is real. I'm over 50. Since Dan left me, I'm a great deal more haggard looking than I was before. It's not as though I'll have employers beating down the door for me.

Since Dan left, I also haven't been able to write a word except for this journal, so my book sales have tanked, too. I'm late on my next book. I haven't even started it. And I completely don't care. I'm so overwhelmed with living my own nightmare, I can't focus on imaginary characters with problems that are now much smaller than my own. It's not as though I will be able to depend on that income. Just when you think you have everything planned . . . life happens. Or in this case, death.

# # #

Hindsight: Finances. I can't stress enough the importance of a rational mind when you're trying to make decisions that will have a financial impact on your future. Regarding the state health plan, I only had 30 days to make an expensive 'yes or no' decision. And Jesus— what a thirty days they were. The first, nightmarish month after the death of my life partner. It's hard to make huge decisions when you've suffered a catastrophe. If there is any way to put off your decisions of magnitude, my recommendation is to kick the can down the road a few months. Even now, decisions now are still difficult, but in the first thirty days, you're nearly paralyzed. Grief. Terror. Overwhelm. It's not the time to be making life altering decisions. I'm not saying decisions are easy now, but it is *easier* at the six month point or the one-year point to find lucid moments when you will be better able to make a rational decision. The *initial* shock has worn off. At the ten-day point, the twenty-day point, I was barely functional.

My expensive health care decision may have been the *wrong* decision, but I tried to think it through logically— all while not knowing what the future would bring. Luckily, I work in benefits, so I had the comfort of familiarity with what I was analyzing. I ran the numbers. My assumptions: a large state plan would likely not experience volatile spikes in rates. In fact, I made the bet the state plan would remain very stable, so the monthly cost I was committing to would likely not change much over three to five years. In hindsight, I've been right—so far. If there's any logic to be found when you make your decision, try to invoke it. If you know someone who can help you read through the information, take advantage and phone a friend.

We are all weakened financially (and in every other way) when our loved one dies. Dan had always planned to retire at 62 and then work part time at something more fun. Instead, he died at fifty-six. Financially, I have now lost six years of income. Six years of 401k saving for the future. Six years lopped off the pension he would have received if he'd lived. I also now have an extra $ 600 per month in health insurance expense.

Our spouses dying drastically young is not something we can typically prepare for. When the unthinkable *does* happen, we must be hyper aware of the decisions we make, weighed against how long we now face paying for life on our own. Try not to make an impulsive decision that can impact you worse than the body blow you've already been dealt. We can only do the best we can, with the knowledge and assets we have in place at the time the worst happens.

# # #

Part Two:

"It is fortunate we have no choice in life. Because it means you must move forward." Audrey Hepburn

6 months: The Widows I've enrolled in a grief therapy group that begins in a couple weeks. I am eager to start. I know I am pinning a great deal of hope on an external source— as though just by going, it will somehow make Dan's death less awful to bear. Nine weeks of group therapy working through his death will somehow make it easier? My rational mind knows this can't possibly be the case, but after six months without him here, I've become a little less rational. About hope and fear and pain and grief. In some ways I just want the awfulness to go away. I want something in my life to feel "normal" again. Whatever normal can possibly feel like now. Will normal be more of what I've already experienced? Coming home each night alone? Heating up leftovers? Reading the paper and then watching too much TV? Because even though I've gotten used to that part, I'm not a huge fan. It's too quiet. It's lonely. The days stretch endlessly into one another, the only marker being 'weekend' or not.

Let's face it, even if the therapy group works, my new normal is still one without my best friend. But, at this point I'm so tired of being sad all the time. Of feeling overwhelmed. Of being afraid. Alone. Angry that he's gone. Angry that other lesser human beings are still here. Frightened of what my life now looks like without him in it. Of it being just me. Getting older by myself. Alone. We were supposed to do that together. Dan helping me; me helping him. Now, I'm scrounging rides to my colonoscopy appointment because I don't have anyone to take the day off with me. Already, I can see that I'm going to become an annoyance. To those people with lives. To people who have someone to help them. I've entered the afterthought zone. I'm the person no one wants to end up like. The person who represents "there but for the grace of God go I". While I wait for lord knows how long before I get to see Dan again, part of me still wishes for it to be right now.

But then I have to think about why I'm still here. There has to be a reason, right? The girls need me because I'm the only parent left. Because they've been dealt a blow to the safe, secure, loving life they've lived until he left us in March. And I, of course, desperately need them. But we raised them right. They are remarkable young women with bright futures, doing work they enjoy. They've each found a beautiful, kind, intelligent man to share their lives with. Our work here is done. Should I still be lingering at a party when I'm not really needed? Will I become that in-the-way mom who has no life? The one they *need* to invite to events because they feel sorry for me? That's never a role I wanted to imagine for myself.

The other part of me cringes over what it would do to the girls if I left them too—at least now. They've been through so much. I also grieve over how much of their lives I would miss. One of us has to be here to bear witness to the lives of the beautiful girls we created.

I was reading something last week, Helen Keller, I think. She said something to the effect of "if you stare too long at the door that has closed to you, you could end up missing the door that has opened". Thus far, I don't believe I've found any open doors, or even windows. We've had too much rain for that this summer. But, if there's any chance Ms. Keller could possibly be right, I feel I need to start seeking out the draft that will guide me to my open door. Maybe it's that broken window out on the shed.

Anyway, since I probably need to stick around for a while, I find myself pinning a great deal of hope on these upcoming grief therapy sessions. I'm sure they will disappoint in some way, if only because my expectations are so utterly unrealistic. I want to come away feeling normal. Confident, as I move forward without Dan. I'd like to believe I can be happy again. That our girls will recover stronger than ever and I can play a role in their happy lives. That's what I hope. And if Dan's somewhere up there watching us, I know he's rooting for that too. So, we'll see how the sessions go. I'll report back later.

On another note, I've met with yet another investment advisor (number 3) to run some scenarios to determine what shape I'm in financially and what I need to do to prepare for the future on my own. It has been interesting to hear different opinions on what steps I should/could take; comparing them to the ideas I've had; the worries I have for the future; the money I have to work with. You get the idea.

On a positive note, this one is suggesting I'll be okay if I continue working for at least six years or so. That is largely a result of Dan's and my combined efforts. All those years of saving for the future instead of spending in the moment. It still infuriates me that Dan will never reap any rewards from all that hard work and oftentimes the miserable circumstances he faced while doing so. Unlike my co-workers, Dan worked with some pretty selfish people. It always seemed unfair to me that a job with such great benefits had to come with such a petty, lazy 'team'. A team of one-trick-ponies taking advantage of a seriously broken state system. Where deadbeats rule and hard workers get punished. If there's anything to be thankful for, it's that he no longer has to face that each day.

While my work was more pressured, I've been so fortunate to work with wonderful people. We are truly a family. Sometimes dysfunctional, but always caring about each other. At the end of the day, maybe I won't live long enough to enjoy the benefits of our diligent thirty-six years of saving either. No big deal—we leave it to the girls and their kids. Either way, it's better than not having enough. For as awful as the last six months have been, I haven't had to experience the overwhelming stress of not having enough money to pay our bills.

I also made that decision to pay off the girls' student loans. It was a big chunk of what Dan left, but now I'm proud that we— that *he*—paid off their college loans. Something that would have taken them another decade to achieve. *Dan* did it for them. That's his legacy. I think he would be proud.

I'll still be stressing about how to pay for weddings when the time comes, but for now I need to take it one day at a time and concentrate on getting through each day. I've also taken steps to preserve our assets in the event I'll need nursing home care later on. I've tried to clean up my finances so it's easier on the girls if something should happen to me. Death has a way of opening your eyes to all the things we tend to put off. With that in mind, I'm trying to not put off the important stuff that could make the girls' lives harder if I end up going like Dan did, without any warning. I've never had to think like that before, but now that I am, I'm probably going off the deep end trying to prepare for it.

I'm in planning mode, which would have likely driven my husband crazy. He was the "will you stop worrying? We're good!" person. And I played the role of "but what if—". So, I'm falling back on what's natural to me, but I'm trying to mix in a little Dan spontaneity. In that light, the girls and I are planning the heck out of a trip to Italy scheduled for next summer. We'd always talked about a trip together, but now it has all become so much more urgent: like something we *need* to do instead of just talking about it. So, Dan and I are going to cover the tab on that, too. It will be expensive. A giant splurge. The sort of splurge we would historically have talked ourselves out of. But this time, I sorta don't care that it's impractical. I can pay for it out of my book income this year, which would normally go for logical, practical things like savings and 401k and paying down the girls' student loans.

When I have a faltering moment of worry, I think about all the trips Dan and I will never take together and then I don't care so much about the expense. Before they're engaged and married and having babies, the girls and I need to do this. It's what I'm still here for. What I'm working for each day. So, we're going to make it happen. Hopefully, Dan would be proud of us and not too worried about the money. Although—I did stop Friday to buy a mega millions ticket because the jackpot was 338 million, so I've got that going for us, too. We'll have nothing to worry about!

# # #

Hindsight: So, the trip we planned was extremely fortuitous. More about it later, but it was literally a dream come true for us. We spent a wonderful vacation in glorious Italy. The timing ended up being only six months before the global pandemic hit and shut down all travel. The places we visited in Italy ended up being so hard hit by the virus. It was heartbreaking to see, especially so soon after we'd visited there. But, two years later, I am so thrilled we got to take that trip. You never know what life is going to throw at you. So, if you have a trip in your heart—you should take it as soon as everything finally opens up once again. I will never regret it. And I vow to do it again sooner rather than later.

Hindsight 2: More about money and possibly more important: organization skills. Dan and I had set up a half-hearted spreadsheet of all our passwords and account numbers. I would have said that we'd thought of "pretty much" everything. However, that did not turn out to be the case. For anyone who has had to spend an hour on the phone with (insert your Pain-In-The-Ass-Cable-Provider) here, you know what I'm talking about.

Some of our monthly bills were set up in my name. Some were in his. There was no rhyme or reason to them. All the annoying accounts *somehow* ended up being in Dan's name, probably because thirty-five years earlier, I'd had the genius foresight to say 'honey, why don't *you* call the cable company?' knowing his infinite patience with them would be an asset after an hour spent imprisoned on hold, whereas my tendency to erupt in a string of obscenities would likely have worked against us in the cooperation department.

Consequently, my password spreadsheet was somewhat of a joke. After Dan died, the girls and I were scrambling as we sifted through his jotted notes so I could try to cancel the sports package that was costing an extra $ 40 per month when there was literally no one home to watch it. It took me five months to get pain-in-the-ass cable to finally agree that he was dead so I could take over the account as administrator. This was after three separate trips to their office on my lunch hour; twenty miles roundtrip.

Twice, I'd provided a copy of the death certificate. I watched them scan it into their system. After they said, "you're good to go" (twice), all the billing did indeed change to my name, but when I tried to go online as administrator—I was STILL denied access. And, of course, refunds for sports packages never viewed "*can't possibly be retroactive. Why—we'd go out of business...*" So, that's $ 200 I'll never get back.

Remember my prediction? If I ever reach the point of complete madness—the cable company will bear the brunt of my wrath. If you hear anything about it, it's definitely me.

Anyway, I digress. Nearly three years later, my password spreadsheet is a thing of beauty. It is a BEAST of organization. I update it several times a year, whenever I realize a scrap of information is missing. I've attached a list in the appendix section just to give you an idea of how you could set one up yourself if you're as appreciative of organization as I am. Please be sure to admire it if you make it to the end of this book.

Hindsight 3: Money: We can only work with what we have. What we earn; what he earned and has left you; pensions; life insurance; what you saved together. I was obsessively worried in the early months after Dan died about cleaning up my finances so I wouldn't leave a mess for our daughters. It was almost as though I could hear a clock ticking—as though the hourglass was running out on my life, too. I had a sense of urgency I'd never felt before. And I couldn't bear the thought of leaving a mess behind.

I started to build a budget based on my income alone; I constructed spreadsheets to calculate potential retirement scenarios. I met with a lawyer to update my will, power of attorney and medical directives. I met with an insurance rep to figure out whether I could afford a long term care plan. Let me tell you—long term care plans are crazy expensive, but if needed, could be a financial godsend to my kids if I end up sticking around too long and they're forced into figuring out how to pay for my care.

While I did all this, heart thudding and in a near frantic state, I eventually did calm down. For me it was so important to *know* this was taken care of. I needed to know the girls would have a neat paper trail in the event I were to die suddenly. Before Dan died, I never felt such a strong sense of urgency, but now that he has, I know it could happen again.

However you tackle the organization monster is obviously what will work for you. But if you have absolutely no idea how to start, just start small. Look at your checkbook or your statement. Try to figure out what you're spending money one. Start with the easy stuff—the things you pay every month. Then widen your range to the things you pay bi-monthly; quarterly; half year property taxes; annual expenses. Then you can start to figure out the rest. How much you spend on groceries; the gym; takeout; etc. Start with the smallest step. Once you complete that, you'll be ready for more. Bottom line: Just do it. Tackle one item at a time and get it done. Like cleaning a closet or your junk drawer. We know they get out of hand, but we have to be in the right mood to tackle them. Soon, you'll be at the point where you're just tweaking your plan, like I finally am.

Planning now is the gift you give your kids and loved ones so their time grieving you isn't complicated with overwhelm at the paperwork mess you've left behind. Think about creating a budget. It can be simple at first. Dan was the accountant in the family, but luckily, I paid all the bills. If you just don't feel able to start now, at least consider revisiting it. Seeing on paper your expenses versus your income can either be startling or comforting. Either way, we need to know those numbers, right? We may need to start making a few course corrections before we get into trouble. I happen to like planning. I like looking at different options. There are numerous financial and budgeting apps available that will help you do the same thing, Please take advantage of them. If not for you, then for the person who will be trying to figure it out later.

# # #

6.5 months: **Loneliness** We talk about loss as though it is static. Someone was here. The person died. They are no longer here. And that's about it. If you're not directly affected, your thoughts likely progress no further. We can imagine what someone is feeling, but we can't truly know (trust me—you're lucky).

The reality is that loss is fluid. It is constantly changing, taking on new shapes. Never forgotten, it is something merely adapted to. In the early days, this stage involves a great deal of pain. Gut-wrenching. Heartbreaking. Stab-you-in-the-chest. Panic-inducing. It changes constantly. One minute, you're okay. Either not thinking about it or avoiding it or just at peace for a brief moment in time. The next minute, you're crying. Over absolutely nothing or over something excruciatingly specific. Like the flash of his smile or the memory of his arms around you. Sometimes his picture makes me smile. Other times I can't bear to look at them.

But now, as I trudge upstairs to bed, through a too silent house, I realize in the stillness that it's now been half a year of quiet. Half a year of climbing these stairs. Alone. And that six more months from now, I'll be doing the same thing. And the thought crosses my mind how can I possibly do this for *another* six months?

Then I realize—it's not *just* six more months. It's six more and six more after that and then it's six years; then ten and twenty until my time finally runs out too. Our loss is permanent. Our change is permanent. We didn't just lose our person in the here and now. We lost our future, too. And as I sit here on the edge of our bed, I wonder what could possibly be the purpose of all this sorrow? Another night not sleeping? Of feeling I failed him. Of missing him. Of wishing he would just come back. Another day dragging to work late because when I do finally fall asleep it's nearly time to get up again. And I am left trying to grasp my role. To understand my purpose. What is the reason I'm still here? If I ever find the answer to that— will it even help?

I've officially entered the stage of "he would've". He would've loved that the Red Sox clinched their division early. He would've been over the moon knowing they kicked the Yankees' asses (Skankees in our house—Sorry, not sorry.) to win the AL East. He would've laughed so hard to see Alex Rodriguez dressed in a Red Sox uniform after losing a bet.

Someone asked me yesterday if I was watching the games. If I was taking pleasure in something Dan would have enjoyed so damned much. But I can't watch any of it. All it does is remind me of him. Of us. Staying up crazy late to watch the 2004 series. Each game going thirteen innings. Each game like giving birth. And each one something he cherished. Each inning he was living and dying with every pitch. That night of the last World Series game? We woke the girls up and made them get out of bed. Chelsea was protesting, rightfully so—that she was tired. Dan, however, didn't care. He *made* her get up to watch. She was complaining about an algebra test the next day and he *still* made her get up! He explained to our grumpy daughter that it would be historic. And more important, it would be part of *our* family history and that she had to bear witness to it.

Soon, she and Miranda were wide awake, celebrating with him as the Sox finally won. I still remember how amazed they both were when our phone began ringing off the hook at 1:30 in the morning. Their faces suggested they couldn't quite understand how momentous the occasion was. How much that win was a part of their dad.

Years later, they still talk of it. Of being glad he went a little crazy that night. Glad he'd insisted. Glad he'd shaken them awake and made them come downstairs to watch with us. Hopefully someday, it will be something we can all talk about and laugh. Smile. Remember fondly. But right now . . . it's too soon to talk about happy times. It's too real that he's missing it this year. That he'll never know about it.

"No," I answered my friend as I fought tears thinking about it. I can't watch now. As much as Dan might want me to. I can't watch the Red Sox. I can't watch the Patriots. I can't watch the team from Washington. The Washington thing isn't exactly a hardship. They still usually suck. And damned if UVA isn't winning this year. They beat Miami last night and all I could think about were all the games over the past dozen years Dan attended with his friend, when Virginia would lose most of the time; often in a big, painful way. How much they'd both spent on games that were so painful to watch—and now, they finally win. Now they look like a cohesive team playing something recognizable as football. Games Dan would have enjoyed attending. And instead of joy— or the old "he's watching from heaven" crap, all I feel is cheated. Screwed over on his behalf because he should have been here to rejoice in it all. 56 was too young to go. My 85-year-old mother still gets to watch football each Saturday and Sunday and my Dan—30 years younger, is gone.

I was at a conference this past week, feeling distinctly alone in Dallas, despite several of my colleagues being in attendance. They knew what had happened to me and were sad on my behalf; comforting to talk with; yet all I could think about was my empty house back home. The text messages I wasn't getting from Dan. One of the women broke away to take a call from her husband back home and I nearly doubled over with the realization there was no one for me to check in with. No one who was missing me. That my 'home' is just an empty house I cling to because of the memories. Because it is familiar in this terrible new, unfamiliar world. It's all I have left of him. Of us. In those moments, I felt more alone than if I'd been with strangers.

It's odd to feel as though you're on an island by yourself. People pass by in boats; they wave; some drift in to visit the island; to cheer you up and check to see that you're okay. But, even while you're so thankful to see them; eternally grateful for their company; for their understanding; their thoughtfulness—at some point you're wishing to be alone again, if only so you can just break down and cry in peace. You need them and you love them. But you know they can't stay.

At some point, everyone must leave. Back to their own busy, happy lives. You know they can't truly make yours better. They can only make it bearable for a brief moment before they leave you. In a strange, counterintuitive way, it's almost easier if they never stopped by to visit your island in the first place. Because when they aren't there, you're numb. You're lonely, but you're familiar with it. You've grown accustomed to being alone. And when you're blessed by a visit with someone you love, somehow—you're already thinking about how you'll feel when they leave and you're dreading the parting.

You are reminded of the quiet you'll face at the end of a wonderful visit—rather than enjoying the moments of the actual visit. Appreciating their presence. I pray this feeling won't last, or I'll end up even more isolated than I've already become.

At one point, my conference group was talking about empathy (we're all HR people) and how they rarely cry at anything. I said nothing, while silently acknowledging that I used to be like that, too. Not without empathy, but accustomed to remaining neutral—having witnessed the gamut of human emotion play out around us. Maybe we get hardened to it because we usually have to deal with the worst; clean up the ugliest messes. We can't be helpful to our employees if we're falling apart along with them. We need to be the strong ones. The practical ones. The women (mostly) who help them clean up whatever unfortunate mess our employees find themselves in. We are the people who assist them in enduring whatever crisis is playing out in their lives.

But, in that moment with my colleagues, all I could think was, they should drop to their knees and pray to God they don't lose their person—because they'll soon be crying all the time. Over everything and nothing. They will become like me. A quiet, despairing, emotional wreck—with the increasing suspicion it might never get any easier.

# # #

6.5 months: My Odd Relationship With My House There are terrible days. And there are bearable days. Thus far I haven't experienced a truly happy day— unless the girls are home. Then it's a grateful, relief-filled happy, tinged with sadness. I'm so thrilled to see them; to spend time together; to pray the time with them crawls instead of flies. But, at the same time, that very togetherness we all crave is a heartbreaking acknowledgement that our lives have been permanently altered. The loving family we have always been will never be the same again.

It doesn't mean I don't have hope for the new unit we've become. Because I do. Even in the depths of my despair, I try to look to the future. To a day when we'll finally all be closer together. To a day when I don't have to dread their leaving because we'll be ten miles apart instead of three hundred. When there will be the overwhelming comfort of just *knowing* they're close by. That it won't be months before our next visit, but days. I am counting the weeks on the calendar until the magic date when we can collectively release the breath we've been holding— to acknowledge we've *made it*. To the other side.

After stumbling through the longest, darkest tunnel we will ever know, we will finally see the faintest glow of sunlight. On that magical day, we will glance back over our shoulders. We will acknowledge the receding darkness, we will wince at the million shards of broken glass we have crawled through, our hands and knees still bloody as we emerge. We will stare at each other and realize we're still whole. Battered and bruised, but confident we can finally heal. Still aching over our loss, but no longer flattened by sorrow.

I long for the day when the gaping hole in my heart is finally scarred over. When I experience a twinge of pain instead of a knife blade. The day I can embrace my memories instead of steering away from them. Because thus far, not thinking about him is equally as painful as thinking about him. The day I break the cycle of tears, tissues, blinding headache and falling into bed will be a good one. I know that day is out there. Currently beyond my reach, but it's on the horizon. I may not be able to see it yet on the calendar, but I have faith that day exists.

I have faith in my girls and I have faith in me. Not all the time, mind you. But today, I do. Because I am strong and I am stubborn and I cannot give up on us. As a woman who loved her husband deeply, my worst fear has already been realized. My nightmare scenario has already played out. I have loved and lost the greatest person I'll ever know. The only thing remaining is to press on. To help our daughters move forward. To live and love and celebrate their lives. To always remember how good he was; to remember how much of Dan's kindness and joy and humor still resides inside them.

We have an obligation to live the life he always wanted for us. I cannot afford to wallow. Even if it made me feel better (it doesn't), it's not how I want to spend the rest of my life. For now, I will continue to plod forward, one day at a time, marking each week; each month until we arrive at that day. The new normal we will finally have made our peace with.

A strange phenomenon I've experienced recently: I've had to travel for business this month, something I normally look forward to. But this time, as the dates approached, I grew nervous over leaving my house for four days each time. My big house would be empty. Not unlike how it is each night as I roam it. But all of a sudden, I was looking at it from the perspective of it being my safe place. When I lock myself in each night, it's MY place. Both familiar and foreign. Both soothing and painful. Comforting and startlingly quiet. But, when I leave, it's like I'm abandoning the only friend I have left. While I travel, I'm alone, a thousand miles away, in an unfamiliar city and my house— the only comforting thing I have left that feels remotely like my old life, is dark and quiet and alone. No one there to breathe even a short, rasping breath of life into it.

Once I return, I am flooded with relief to be back in familiar territory— yet I'm also sad again. Because I'm alone in this giant, empty house. As soon as I'm away, I want to be home again. But as soon as I'm home, I am smothered by my aloneness. What gives? Will I ever feel comfortable again?

# # #

7 months: I'm '*Okay*' It's Halloween. I've spent a great deal of time lately wondering whether Dan's death was preventable. After 36 years together— shouldn't I, above all others have seen the signs? He'd looked tired the last couple months. His job had become a ball buster, as opposed to the safe haven a state job should be. Unless your one-trick pony coworkers with too little to do, enjoy making life difficult for others. He'd been increasingly miserable. Getting all the problem employees "shifted" to his team. The ones no one else wanted. The ones who would've been fired long ago, had they worked in the private sector. But at the state, they were basically safe for life. Or retirement. In one breath he was exhausted by the drama. In the next, he was excited and relieved for the trip he'd planned for the week after he died. He was going to Atlantic City. To gamble, to walk and to just enjoy a week away from the pressure cooker hellhole his job has become.

My husband was a pack mule type of employee; used to bearing a heavy load; used to responsibility and hard work. In fact, he preferred it that way. Adjusting to the state job mentality had been a difficult transition nine years earlier. Working around problem employees; always having to document everything in case someone decided to pitch a fit or make a false accusation— of favoritism; of non-favoritism; of being female, of being Black or Brown or White.

He was expected to monitor their time, because despite their having 6-8 weeks off each year, his employees pissed it away as though vacation days were a bag of chips. Never able to stop taking days off;

so much that they would actually run out of time before year end. He had to document because they consistently "forgot" to acknowledge vacation days on their timesheets. Dan's boss insisted he keep track of every day off; every late arrival—which with a staff of six, literally amounted to every single day. In more than nine years, he'd never experienced one week when all six staff members were present. NOT. ONE. WEEK. You name it and his hostile work environment provided it. Fodder. Rumors. Innuendo. Self-serving lies. Yet, he'd stuck it out, counting the days until his next vacation and the next and the next. Until he would finally be able to retire.

On the Wednesday he died, he worked late that and then dropped dead at the ballgame that should have been his stress relief for the day. He was two days away from his vacation, where he'd vowed to get in 100,000 steps that week.

Dan worked out three times a week— always cardio because he'd always feared a heart attack. His dad had died of a heart attack, too. But at least his father made it to age 64. In addition to his workouts, Dan walked every day at lunchtime. He would easily get 10000 steps a day. Yet somehow, we missed whatever cosmic signs were provided us. Maybe I should have insisted at age 50 that he start seeing a cardiologist annually. But, with life as busy as it is; would that have been feasible? Would he have gone? Would they have discovered he had high cholesterol? Would he have taken the statin that likely would have been prescribed? The man who complained about taking aspirin. The man who didn't even like taking allergy meds? Likely, an annual visit would have detected the massively blocked artery that suddenly killed him seven months ago.

Could anything have saved him? If I'd been paying more attention that night—as opposed to watching the game? When he got up to walk off the "pulled muscle" would those five minutes have saved him? Of course, with no defibrillator available, what would medics have done? The ambulance may have arrived sooner, which might have saved him. When he returned to our seats, he claimed he felt better. Was that his fear talking? Wishful thinking? Prayer? When he looked at me with that strange expression on his face— why didn't I know then? 36 years with him, and I couldn't decipher the look on his face.

I still dream about that night. That last glance. It is a terrible vision. One I can't seem to erase. If I'd actually seen him collapse and die . . . my best friend in the world. The only person who'd truly loved me just the way I am, flaws and all. I can only imagine what nightmares I'd be having now. It's probably awful of me to feel relieved that I didn't witness that. But I can't help it. I don't think I would have made it. I would have died right there beside him. And our kids would have no one here to muddle along on their behalf. Yet, I somehow have to come to terms with the guilt I carry. What few signs there were, I missed them all. And the catastrophic result of that failure may yet destroy me.

A coworker asked me today how I was doing. I, of course said 'I'm okay'. Like how else do you respond to that question? I feel desperately lonely? Hopeless? So sad I sometimes feel as though I'm drowning in it? I'm worried it will never end? No. You maintain a brave face. You say, "I'm fine" and you change the subject. He asked, "what has been the hardest thing for you to get used to?" I stared at him, both fascinated and horrified by his question—one he'd truly meant no harm in asking.

Finally, I answered. "Everything. Everything is the hardest thing to get used to". It's the stark truth. Every waking moment provides some level of pain. Each moment requires a level of strength and endurance I didn't know I had. Some moments are excruciating.

Some are merely hard. Very rarely, a moment feels easier. Right now? I'm late going back to work from lunch because I sat here typing this and crying instead of eating. I'll have to redo my makeup before I head back. Try explaining *that* to any sane person. I'll go back to work drained; washed out and still hungry because I didn't get the chance to eat. That's a pretty normal day now.

What's the *hardest* thing? Sometimes it's taking a deep breath. Sometimes it's driving down our street. Entering our empty house. Cooking alone. Eating alone. Talking to myself as I force down food I have no interest in. Lying awake most of the night thinking about him. Getting through a workday when you feel dead inside. Trying to summon empathy to care about the rest of the world when your own life has come to an abrupt, screeching halt. But if someone asks, I'll say "I'm okay."

# # #

7 months: Introducing Ginger Big news! I got a cat. She's a rental. After coming home to an empty house every day for seven months, I walked in one night and just lost it. That moment, I decided I couldn't face another minute alone in this house. I went online and completed the application to foster a cat from the local humane society. Maybe they were desperate, but I heard from them the next day! The last couple years Dan was here, we'd agreed to a no more pets policy so we'd be free to travel and not have to care for other living things, aside from our kids. I wasn't thrilled about it, but he'd good naturedly put up with us having a family pet for at least twenty years, so he'd earned a break.

Along with that agreement, we'd also to grow old together, take lots of trips and spoil our grandchildren. Clearly, we have trouble keeping our promises.

So, now I have a loaner cat to attempt to fill the hole in my heart. Her name is Ginger. She's a beautiful striped, orange tabby. I picked her up last week, the day before Halloween. If she were my real cat, I'd probably have renamed her something adorable, like Pumpkin or Marmalade and I'd call her Marmie for short. But, since I won't be keeping her, I didn't really think much about her name. So, she's Ginger (which is also super cute, BTW). She's getting to know me. I'm getting to know her. I don't want to commit to a permanent cat because Miranda now says she's moving home next March once her lease is up. And she already has two wild, fun boy cats, so our house will go from zero to crazy the moment the Frat Boys arrive.

If it's anything like when she was in grad school and we had to take the Frat Boys in for a few months while she was gone for an internship, we'll have our hands full with just Griffey and Sebastian. I'm so thrilled to know she's moving back, but it is still an endless five months away and I can't bear another minute of being so desperately lonely. So, now I have Ginger. I'll take care of her until someone decides to adopt her. I have promised to bring her to the adoption stand every two weeks. Likely, she won't be living here very long. And she'll certainly be gone by the time the drunken, rowdy Frat Boys arrive.

This is a good test run for me. If it turns out I'm good at fostering, then I'm thinking maybe I'll continue to be a foster mom once Miranda lands on her feet and moves back out. I'm going to need some hobbies to fill my time.

Most nights, Ginger and I settle in on the couch like an old married couple. Usually, I just cry while I watch TV. Ginger sits there patiently. Not cuddling, but not judgmental either. She's quietly supportive as I weep and blow my nose. Occasionally, she'll grumble a bit when she's had enough of my sobbing noises. She's chatty, but succinct.

As we hang out together, I'm curious why Ginger hasn't been adopted. She's only about two years old. Her adoptability issue may have something to do with her no-nonsense expression. Unfortunately, she's got a touch of Resting Bitch Face going on. Yet, she is so sweet and loving. She's truly not bitchy at all. The looks I get suggest I should try to get a better handle on myself with the sobbing—but her eyes also suggest she'll forgive me if I promise to try harder.

When I picked her up at the store, she'd been living there in a cage for at least a month. The volunteers told me Ginger had been bullied by other cats in her last foster home, so they'd been forced to remove her, but then they'd been short on foster homes so she'd had to live in the pet store while waiting for the weekend adoption stands. Clearly, she's been through some stuff. She's a little battered and cautious, but at this point, I am, too. We should get along fabulously.

# # #

Hindsight: Looking back from the three-year point, I can honestly say this was a turning point for me. I acknowledged my misery and instead of continuing to wallow and hope for change, I acted to change it. It wasn't exactly a spur of the moment decision, but it was close. I deliberately didn't overthink it, because let's face it. Taking on foster pets is easy to talk yourself out of. You're buying potential problems. Why does no one want these animals? But I'd reached the point that I didn't care what I was about to get into. Making the commitment to take in a living thing that would rely solely on me meant I was ready to commit to being here. To acknowledge that the horrible, life-altering event that happened would not take me out, too. Helping Ginger helped me. I was no longer completely alone. I had someone who was happy to greet me at the door each night. I had company for the first time in seven months. This may sound crazy, but I didn't know how desperately I needed someone/something to take care of. For me, Ginger was my new start. A new routine. A tiny bit of normal in a stormy sea of unknowns. Fostering may not be for everyone, but for me, it began my journey back to discovering what a *new normal* could possibly look like. I am grateful every day for that impulsive decision to commit to caring for her.

# # #

7.5 months: Can We Be Happy Again? Today I'm still lying in bed and I'm reflecting on how grief changes you. It's mid-term election time (2018) and everyone is stressed over the utter decline of civility. I read an article about the psychology behind the anxiety we all feel now. The meat of the article was that even though we think about it, we really won't all move to Canada if the midterms turn out to be as much of a disaster as the 2016 election. Psychologically, there's a term for how we *think* we'll feel after an upheaval versus how we actually end up feeling. And the gist is that as bad (or good) as we feel in the moment of a life altering event, we all eventually revert back to a baseline level of happiness. So, if you were an upbeat, happy person before a tragedy, then theoretically, you will eventually return to that upbeat, happy person as the distance between you and the tragedy becomes greater.

Although this article was talking about the horror that American politics has devolved to, and as a comparison, the happiness one would likely feel after a substantial lottery win, I couldn't help but to apply this theory to my own situation. Seven plus months after my husband died, this article has given me the slightest glimmer of hope to learn that our bodies are physically programmed to return to a mean. And not that I was a raving optimist before his death (that was more Dan's role) but I was a generally happy person with normal ups and downs. If this article was correct, then maybe someday I will return to that state.

For now, I liken my grief to a car wreck. My vehicle thru life hit a wall last March. Out of nowhere, a brick wall appeared in my path. I hit it going full speed. No chance to brake. Somehow, I emerged from the smoldering wreckage of twisted steel. Instead of being slashed by the sharp metal; instead of bleeding to death from the explosion of broken glass, my injuries are largely invisible. My injuries are internal. Crushed organs, traumatic soft tissue injuries that have left me destroyed from the inside, reverberating out to the surface. My heart is now where my stomach used to be. Even though I may look normal on the outside; my insides know differently.

I finally understand the meaning of the term 'brave face' when you could literally be dying inside, but on the surface, you look fine. Normal. Strong. I guess in that sense, grief is like any other mental or emotional illness. The reality is that we never really know what another person is enduring behind their eyes. Behind their smile. Are we all experiencing some level of pain? I've heard the Robert Service quote, also attributed to Muhammad Ali: *everyone walks with a pebble in their shoe.* Are we all just hobbling through life in a state of quiet despair?

Is grief just part of the deal? In trade for a mostly good life, must we agree to endure horrific, life-altering consequences at some point? Times when our luck simply runs out? Are there times when it's merely *our turn* to experience a years-long period of profound and utter sadness? When we emerge from our prospective tunnels of grief and sadness (assuming we do emerge), are we relieved? Grateful it's over? Bitter we were forced to endure such unimaginable pain? More understanding of ourselves and others? A little (or a lot) more introspective? Or do we just appreciate everything a little more? I would love to know the answers to some of these questions. Asking for a friend.

# # #

7.5 months: Hallmark Widows I now watch far more TV than I used to. Or maybe I just watch different channels now. I no longer have to battle for the remote nor debate the merits of the fiftieth baseball game that week compared to just about anything else. Consequently, I've been watching a lot of Hallmark channel, mostly in the background as I try to regain my focus on reading (which so far, isn't working), Anyway, after watching about thirty of these movies, I've decided I want to be a Hallmark channel widow instead of a widow in real life.

Hallmark widows are all so perfect. Handsome widowers, beautiful widows. The beauty sort of goes without saying. They are actors, of course. There are lots of scenes of these attractive people 'thinking deep thoughts'. Brooding introspectively—but they rarely ever cry. No snotty, red nose and packed sinuses. No requisite pile of used tissues; no blotchy skin or red eyes to contend with. No sobbing so much you swear you're going to crack a rib. This time of year, the Hallmark widows are all closed-off to the idea of celebrating Christmas. Despite their lack of spark, they always seem to have a beautifully decorated home (by Balsam Hill, judging by the numerous commercials) and a requisite adorable child or two—basically unscarred by the loss of their other parent. *Enough* time has always passed.

Sidebar: how much time is *enough* time? Two years? Three years? Four? Obviously, it's different for every widowed person in real life with numerous contributing factors. In Cedar Falls or Maple Heights or Codfish Cove, it seems like the average is 18 months to about 4 years. Anyway, Hallmark kids are surprisingly well adjusted instead of traumatized. No matter their age, they never seem to want gifts for themselves. No, the Hallmark kids are laser focused on simply finding the magical person who can bring a smile back to their *grieving* parent's face.

Wouldn't it be nice if grief were actually that simple? Seriously—sign me up. That you could feel better about yourself after only two hours? Or eighteen months? I'm not mocking the skill of the actors nor the stories. I love Hallmark. I'm merely wishful thinking. Can I please have Hallmark grief instead of the real kind? The kind that ambushes you. The kind that leaves you sobbing at the drop of a hat. The grief you experience where you wander through stores that are gloriously decorated for the holiday you can no longer bear to contemplate. The gorgeous ornaments that make you pause for a moment; touch them; contemplate buying them for the tree . . . until you remember. This year, there won't be a tree. Then you reel back from the sledgehammer blow to your heart when you remember this Christmas will be the suckiest, most horrible holiday you've ever imagined. You try not to break down in the middle of the ornament aisle before you can retreat to the safety of your car and finally lose it privately.

This year, there's no point in decorating. It's not as though it will make me feel better. For me, being surrounded by cheer makes me feel worse. Hopefully, future years will be less awful, but all I can hope for this year is to get through the holidays as quickly and quietly as possible. My grief therapy group assignment this week is to think about how I will get through the holidays and then plan for them. Our therapist says that having a plan can help us feel more in control. She alleges it will help us get through all the other milestones I'm dreading in the coming year. I've already made it through our wedding anniversary, but now they're starting to pile up like obstacles in the road and they're so close together, I fear I'm going to careen into one and blow a tire.

My birthday was this week— which Dan and I never really made a big deal about. We'd maybe go to dinner. But at work, I could sense everyone was concerned about me. Seriously, these people I work with are some of the most thoughtful, caring people I will ever have the good fortune to know. I felt an almost hyper awareness around me that day. As though everyone was watching out for me. They bought flowers; they took me to lunch; they made me a giant cake. It was such an overwhelming display of caring that I felt embarrassed. At the same time, I was truly touched by their concern for me. When I got home that night after work, there was a gift bag by my door, left by my beloved neighbor to show that she, too, had remembered.

It left me feeling grateful that night instead of sad. Sometimes when you feel most alone, you can be surprised by how much people care.

For my grief group assignment, I forced myself to think about the rest of this calendar year. Thankfully, I will spend Thanksgiving and Christmas with my daughters. We will try hard to make them fun. We will be exceedingly thankful to be together, but all the while, we will be working to avoid acknowledging the gaping hole Dan's absence will cause. Thanksgiving may be worse than Christmas because that was my husband's birthday, too. It was always my favorite holiday. The family was always together to celebrate with him. There was no rush to decorate or shop for gifts. All of that was in the distant future. Those four days at Thanksgiving were about family time. Hanging out. Sleeping in. Making pumpkin bread once the turkey was in the oven. Watching the parade in our pajamas. Eating too much. Watching college football. Napping without guilt. This year, Dan would've been 57. Would. Have. Been. Whenever I acknowledge his age, it depresses me. For someone so young and so full of life to no longer be here. Who's going to help me wrestle the turkey into the oven?

So, we will make the best of these holidays, and we will pray that next year will be more bearable. Some of my answers to my homework assignment will have to be "I don't know", at least for now. I don't know what we'll do, if anything, for the anniversary of his death. Is it a day I'll ever want to observe? Or will it always be one I slink away from? Will I avoid thinking about it? Will I be relieved when it's over because I've survived it? Or will it be as traumatic as the actual date? The one-year anniversary of the day my wonderful life ended. Having to acknowledge the absolute permanence of this change. Will I choose to ignore it? Will I be strong enough to want to do something to honor his memory? Or will I want to race past that day, too. So that we can finally stop saying "the first *fill-in-the-blank*".

How can I possibly know right now? At nearly eight months into this, I'm different today than I was two months ago. And that was different from four months ago. And six. When you have marked time in days and weeks, four months from now seems so far away. Part of me will just be relieved when it's over. The day of his death is not a milestone I'll ever want to celebrate.

At least by next March, the Hallmark widows will be in the throes of a spring fling. Dan died a few days before Easter. He is risen. Can't get much more biblical than that. I hope for Dan's sake the Easter thing bumped him to the head of the line for Heaven. Back here on Earth, it earmarks Easter as yet another holiday I'll never enjoy again. But at least by then, Hallmark will have pulled us through the bleakness of winter. A Hallmark Spring will celebrate young love; renewal; rebirth, growth—even for their perfect widows. A Hallmark spring will bring a slew of new widows with their precocious kids wanting mommy to have a husband again—and doesn't that lonely tulip farmer look awfully nice? You know what? Sign me up. I'm sure I'll be watching.

Hopefully by then, I'll be feeling a sense of something new. Accomplishment? Exhaustion? Relief? Or just another haggard year older? I don't think Hallmark makes movies about widows like me. I'm betting wretched despair doesn't sell well on a Saturday night. And truthfully, I wouldn't want to watch that, either. I'd rather watch a widow with perfect makeup, good hair and no eye bags. It gives me something to strive for.

# # #

Hindsight: Something really cool I learned from my buddy, Hallmark. I was watching the Hallmark Mystery channel and the story was about stolen identities. The gist of the mystery was that a crime syndicate was stealing the details of deceased people and establishing new identities to make fraudulent real estate purchases. Aurora Teagarden was hot on their trail and ended up hunting down women (widows) to figure out why their husbands were still making transactions. The cops working the case explained to the widows (and to me as I sat there completely dumbfounded) that when a loved one dies, if you don't notify the credit bureaus of their death, their identities can be stolen, and we (the widow) would likely never know.

If you're like me, I'd given zero thought to Dan's credit after he passed away. As we're all well aware, there are ten million other stressors pressing in on you when you lose a loved one. Contacting the credit bureaus will likely always be at the bottom of the list (if it makes the list at all). Truthfully, this was not on my radar. I assumed after the funeral that Social Security would notify the credit bureaus. Many times, they do. But sometimes that information doesn't get registered with the credit bureaus.

You're probably saying, "I never thought of this". Every person I've mentioned this to since watching the movie hadn't heard about the importance of notifying at least one credit bureau. The next day, I googled how to shut down Dan's credit. It was relatively easy. I had to send a quick letter stating his full name, date of death, his birth date, his SS number along with a copy of the death certificate. The process took about two weeks. Three years in, I was able to get his credit shut down and marked as deceased. Once you notify one bureau, they will notify the others for you. So, you only have to contact one. So, a big thank you to my buddy, Hallmark and Aurora Teagarden for such a great, timely reminder. Make sure you eventually take care of this, too. Add it to your list.

# # #

Almost 8 months: Grief Therapy It's Saturday evening. Not even December and it's already getting dark at 5 pm. This was a rough week for whatever reason. My grief group sessions have been both therapeutic and upsetting at the same time. While the expression 'misery loves company' seriously doesn't apply here, the concept of all ten of us sitting there on a cold, rainy Tuesday night for the same reason is somewhat comforting. We are all so very different, yet completely united in our pain. Our bewilderment (most of us) that this has happened to US. To our person. We are united in dread at the approaching holidays. United in the dread of special days like birthdays and anniversaries. All of us squeamish about how to handle the anniversary of our partner's death.

The grief group gives me a great deal to think about and weekly homework to boot. Lots of reading assignments that are equally helpful and depressing. It also leaves me with a residual sadness I carry with me for the rest of the week. The group is doing its job, I suppose, conjuring up questions I would likely keep putting off. Our counselor reminds us in her gently prodding way, that we have so much to work through and that it's better to face it (in our own timeframe) than to bury it, only to have it resurface again and again.

Since this has been an agonizing eight months thus far, the thought of being in this bad shape at year three or four is frightening. So, I am diligently doing my homework each week; forcing myself to talk in the sessions about things I'd rather not revisit, and plodding on each week, all with the hope that a year from now I am incrementally better and a year after that, and a year after that.

On another front, this week was bonus week at work. What I've discovered over the last almost-eight months is that most of the things that used to make me happy or proud or pleased or whatever; now make me sad or numb or, in the best situations, happy for a fleeting moment. This year, receiving the bonus I worked so hard for felt incredibly different. While my company was extraordinarily generous, I felt almost a stab of pain in a moment that should have brought joy or pride or, in some years— relief. That we could pay off a credit card or make a big lump payment on the girls' student loans or pay for next year's beach vacation. This year, I received my check; I went home with it and I had no one to tell. No one I could celebrate the news with. If Dan was still here, we probably would have gone to dinner to celebrate our good fortune.

Sometimes I wonder, were we *too* lucky? Is that why our time together was shortened? I always appreciated Dan. And I know he did me. Something we were never uncertain about was us. Our life. Our love. Our bond. We always knew what we had was better than most people will ever experience. Looking back on it, I wonder if I sort of knew it wouldn't last as long as it should have.

So many times, I would wake in the morning and experience a tremendous pang of relief when I heard him breathing. Why was that? Love? Fear? A subconscious worry? Turns out, the premonitions were accurate. At night, immediately after I return home from work are the times I miss him most. Because I'm home for the day. It's dark and quiet. I used to look forward to coming home. It was our time to catch up on each other's day; to chat over everything and nothing. To make dinner and eat together.

This week Dan would've been so excited for me. So proud. So happy to discuss how much we could give the girls. He would have reminded me (repeatedly) about putting a big chunk in 401k so we could max out for the year. In fact, he would have gone into work the next day and maxed his out through year-end. We were like a well-oiled machine. A team working seamlessly. A dynamic duo. Always on the same page for everything important. Always the same goals. Eyes on our prize of a happy retirement and time with our beautiful girls.

Now, that is gone. This week, I came home and relayed my good news to the foster cat, (who I'm starting to think I might need to adopt). Ginger didn't really care about my bonus. She was happy to see me— which has been a nice change. Someone waiting for me. Talking. Eager to have dinner and sit with me on the couch. Okay— so she's a cat. But it's a serious improvement to my life over the last seven months.

My grief group homework assignment this week was to write Dan a letter. I was dreading it, because thinking about him always makes me cry, but since I cry pretty much every day anyway, why would this be any different? Although I hope he's been aware of what's going on down here, part of me wonders if that is really true. I don't feel his presence the way I'd hoped to. But if Dan doesn't actually know it after nearly eight months of me crying most days, I'll close by saying I really wish he was here.

# # #

Thanksgiving: Am I thankful? Thanksgiving used to be my favorite holiday. Four days off from work. No wrapping or decorating involved. Lots of cooking, but at a relaxed pace. Dan would always make a batch of turkey soup the day after; he enjoyed his time in the kitchen when he could finally have it all to himself. He was the rare man who made a mess and then cleaned it all up himself. Thanksgiving is when we always celebrated Dan's birthday because it falls around the holiday (sometimes on the actual day) and the girls were almost always home. Two years ago, Miranda created a dancing turkey meme with Dan's face on it. We had it made into his birthday cake and it was so funny to see his surprise.

When we were young, it was a fun time to go out with all of our college friends because they'd traveled home for the holiday. Thanksgiving for us has always been a joyous time full of great memories. Which means this week will be a double whammy for a person trying to manage the grief process. I'll be desperately missing him on Thanksgiving and then a few days later I'll get hit again on his birthday. Two days after that will be the eight month anniversary that he's been gone. After that, we get the mac-daddy holiday. Christmas. I can't even think that far ahead right now.

One of our Thanksgiving traditions was to go around the table and ask each person what they are thankful for. I don't know if we will be able to handle that this year. It might send the day into a spiral. The girls didn't want to be at home this year, nor did I. So, this year, we'll be running away. Travelling to meet up with each other. For the very first time, we'll be going out for Thanksgiving dinner. Not exactly the holiday of our dreams, but we have to start somewhere.

What am I thankful for? I'm not sure the middle of a crowded restaurant on Thanksgiving is the best time to ask that question. I will probably break down and cause a snotty-nosed scene. But I have been wondering about it. Can I still be thankful this year? When you lose the love of your life; when it's decades too early; when it's completely without warning; when it punches you in the face with the unfairness of it all— can I truly be thankful for anything? That's my question this week. I'll let you know what I discover.

Thankfulness update: so, we made it through Thanksgiving. It was wonderful seeing the girls. It was also nice to be out of town for the holiday. Being far away certainly wasn't the magic wand that made everything better, because Dan was clearly missing through all of it. However, we still managed to have a lovely time just being together. Dan loved this time of year. Reminders of him were everywhere we wandered. But instead of the memories upsetting us, we seemed able to embrace them. The holiday was also restful because we were all together. There's a certain sense of power I receive when the girls are with me. It's such a rare treat that it's noticeable to me. Of course, once I leave them, I have the downside of a weepy, floundering spiral day because I'm back to being alone again. That bad day is still worth seeing my girls.

I have to confess—part of me wanted to pretend we were all just meeting up for a girls' weekend. I wanted it to be fun because I'm so tired of being sad. Not that the wish actually works that way. We're all still sad. But I'm relieved to learn the girls have good days. They have joy in their lives. They have challenging jobs and amazing, caring boyfriends. I'm glad for them and a little envious of their happiness. But I wouldn't trade the thirty-six years of love and happiness I experienced. It's their turn now.

I'm so glad they are decorating for Christmas even though I can't. While we were together for Thanksgiving, we talked about Dan, of course, but not really "talked". It was almost as though none of us really wanted to venture there. We all knew the days would be difficult, yet we were all determined to try to be happy. After eight months of crying, I figured I could suspend my tears for a few days until I returned home. As part of our pampering, I'd booked massages for the girls and a facial for me. Every time I look in the mirror lately, I feel pretty haggard. After eight months of crying at the drop of a hat, of too little sleep; of stress and grief and the constant battle to stave off depression, I look like hell most of the time. Treating myself to a facial was a relaxing luxury I enjoyed, despite how determined my mind was to wander during the peaceful, quiet time I was supposed to be relaxing.

Dan's brother called Thanksgiving morning, but I hesitated to answer. Instinct told me that speaking with him would set off a chain reaction that might wipe out all of us. Instead, I let his call go to voicemail. He left a lovely message; I'm glad he was thinking of us, but also glad I could just text them later in the day to wish them well. As much as I appreciate people thinking of us, I'm the one who has to endure the call; the conversation; the questions; the "how are you guys doing?" Sometimes those calls cheer me up. But I've also learned that sometimes those calls can spiral me from a passable mood to a sob fest. I could be feeling okay and then after the call, I'm losing it. I never know which way it will go until that moment. Hopefully, the caller understands if I don't pick up, but at this point, I'm the one who has to survive this. I'm learning to be okay with my gut feeling in that moment on the right thing to do.

In answer to my initial question as to whether I am thankful this year, my answer is mixed. I am deeply thankful for my girls and for what little family we have left. I am grateful for the friends who have remained by our sides throughout this nightmare year and who continue to look out for me and care for us. I'm also thankful to be blessed by an amazing group of friends at work who have made this horrible year more bearable and the widows in my group as we all work collectively to learn how to be better alone.

So, at this point, I'm still among the living. Still among the thankful. But check back in a couple days. I may feel differently. Dan's birthday is in two days and two days after that is the eight-month marker that he's been gone. Then, its only 25 days until Christmas. As I stagger to the finish line on this year from hell, I can't decide whether I'll be sad to reach December 31st or relieved to put this year in the rearview mirror. Will New Year's Eve feel like an ending? The official end to the last year he spent here. Or will it be a literal new beginning? More to come on that later.

# # #

November 26: Organ Donation My husband's birthday was today. He would've been 57. For the most part, I blocked it out. It was a busy day at work. Lots of meetings requiring my focus. I managed to get through the day without thinking about it too much. It was hard hearing from people who'd remembered— bringing up the very thing I was trying to forget. At the same time, I was grateful they'd remembered him. Weird, huh? It was so thoughtful of them. To remember. To get in touch. I don't want to sound unappreciative when it was an important day. Yet another milestone I've had to get through.

After work, I went to the gym to work out . . . because that's what I do now. In the futile attempt to stay healthy and alive for the girls. Not that his strict exercise regimen helped Dan any. He was religious about his workouts, swearing it was the differentiator. That tough cardio workouts would protect his heart. That going to the gym would allow him to see his girls through adulthood. He'd vowed he would live longer than his father. And his grandfather before him. But, instead of a longer life, Dan's time on earth ended up being several years shorter than both of them. Ironic, isn't it?

His grandfather only made it to 59. Two uncles also died at 59, but we'd always comforted ourselves that they were high-strung; massively overweight and didn't take care of themselves. His beloved, but chain-smoking-unfiltered-Camels father made it all the way to 64. Dan? Only 56 when he died. So, what was the point of it all? Yet, here I am, at the fucking gym trying to do my part. Walking myself into exhaustion to relieve my stress and hopefully help me start sleeping better.

On his birthday, I managed to make it through the day—all day avoiding the fact that it *was* his birthday. I trudge into the house in the waning hours of autumn, already dark and dreary by the time I left work. I am welcomed by Ginger, who is pleased to see me. I say hello and pet her soft, orange fur, deeply grateful she is there waiting for me in the dark.

An hour later, I finally had time to sift through all the mail that had been held while I was gone for Thanksgiving. There in the pile, I discover a letter from one of Dan's organ donation recipients—thanking me for making the tough decision I was forced to make last spring. A man who is no longer in pain as a result of my husband's donated tissue. I broke down sobbing as I read it—as I do now, writing this entry. Was it Dan reaching out to me on his birthday? If yes, it really sorta backfired.

I honestly don't know how I am supposed to feel. I've felt guilty every time I hear from the donor network. I'm not sure why, but I'd rather not hear from them at all. I don't want to be reminded of the decision I made at the worst moment of my life. His organs weren't mine to give. Would Dan have wanted to be a donor? I don't know. It's not something we ever discussed. Like his cremation. You'd think in 36 years together there would have been literally no conversational stone unturned. Yet, we hadn't talked about cremation. I remember Googling it the morning after he died. Could Catholics be cremated? Because I knew that part would matter to him. But, I also knew I couldn't bury him here when I may not end up *staying* here. I would never be able to bear the thought of leaving him behind if I end up moving in the coming years.

Luckily, it turned out Catholics *can* be cremated, so that's what we ended up doing. But organ donation is a different story. I'm not sure Dan would have wanted that. Really, does anyone ever want to think about someone else owning the organs they're currently using? I seriously believe in organ donation. Why would I want to keep something I can no longer use if it could help someone else? But contemplating it while I'm still in use of them leaves me a little squeamish. It's an unfortunate situation that hospital personnel face every hour. How do we ask this shell-shocked person to make a huge, personal decision when they've just been gut-punched?

In the end, on a horrible night in a clinical, too-bright room, I tried to cut through the jumble of emotions I was feeling—terror being the primary one. In a state of suspended disbelief, I forced myself to concentrate on Dan's generosity. His thoughtfulness. His gentle spirit. He was a shirt-off-his-back kinda guy. He loved helping people, if he could. What would Dan do? Utilizing that perspective, I figured he wouldn't care about his organs, because he would be helping others.

Though I sometimes still feel guilty, I know it was the right decision. But is it wrong that I don't like thinking about it? I don't begrudge the recipients. I'm relieved for them. But—in some ways, I just don't want to know. It doesn't bring me closure or happiness. Maybe someday it will. Maybe in a few years, I'll be grateful that parts of him still live on. That he's still out there, helping others. Easing their pain. Providing the gift of sight through his beautiful, blue eyes. But, for now, hearing from his beneficiaries just starts the cycle of sadness all over again. It takes me back to that awful moment in the hospital when I was forced to make a decision at least a decade too soon. Part of me prays I won't hear from them again. Yet somehow, I know—if I receive another letter, I'll probably open it. And I'll save them for the girls to read someday, if and when it ever becomes less painful.

# # #

8 months and three days: Hello, Iris. I'm fostering another cat now. Unlike Ginger, Iris is a complete basket case. She's been under Miranda's bed for the last two days. I'm not even sure what she looks like. She's dark. I think possibly a tortie. She literally will not come out. I walk in; I place dishes of food on the floor near the bed so she can smell it. I talk to her under the bed and try to coax her out. So far, no dice.

I guess I won't have to worry about wanting to adopt this one. I'm more concerned I may be fostering her for life, because I can't fathom how Iris will ever *become* adoptable. I can't imagine taking this poor, cowering creature to the adoption stand to shrink painfully into the corner of a cage. I can't imagine *catching* her to get her into a carrier to drive her to the adoption stand.

Iris was taken from the home of an elderly lady who died. She had eleven cats, a few of which had to be put down because they were in such bad shape. Not helping matters, Iris has since been bounced around to six different foster homes in six months. She was abused in the last foster home. Another cat terrorized her so much that Iris was peeing under the bed where she lived. The foster family's cat would attack her if she tried to use the litter box. That story is both heartbreaking and a little nerve-wracking. I'm crossing my fingers that Iris won't be peeing under the bed in Miranda's room, but we're already a few days in, so it's kind of too late.

Frankly, I can see why Iris is a basket case. Six strange homes in six months. Eleven cats and an elderly lady before that. At this particular point in my life, I'd say we're shockingly similar in the basket case department. Our worlds have imploded. We don't know where or who we are anymore. Life has treated us very unkindly. We're both shell-shocked. Maybe poor Iris has just had a really terrible year.

I've confirmed (with relief) that she's at least summoning the courage to creep out during the long, silent nights and quiet, still days while I'm at work to use the litter box, so I don't have to contend with her peeing under the bed. At this point, Ginger doesn't even know Iris is in the house. It's just a closed bedroom door to her. We could probably live like this for decades. I guess things could be worse. I'll take care of Iris as long as the humane society needs me to. It's not as though I have a lot of other plans.

# # #

Hindsight: I can honestly say that the fostering process truly saved me in so many ways. I was so unbelievably lonely. After seven months alone, I just knew I couldn't bear it anymore. I'm so glad I sought out the fostering process. Even as I told myself it wasn't a good time because Miranda would be home six months later; I kept going forward with it. As though something inside me knew—*you need this now*. It can't wait another day.

Now, nearly three years later, fostering has received a sudden burst of interest due to the global pandemic. With so many people on lockdown, there have been lots of lonely people testing the waters of pet ownership by agreeing to foster. It truly has been a godsend for all the stray pets out there and it was a godsend to me to have a few furry cats to pamper and care for. Sometimes in our grief we just need a reason each day to get out of bed. Hungry animals will get you out of bed every time. In Ginger's case, she doesn't allow me to sleep in and forget her breakfast. Trust me, you won't want to let them down.

# # #

8.5 months: Friendship It feels as though Dan has been gone forever. And sometimes it feels like it's only been 5 minutes. Sometimes I find myself at work, checking my phone wondering why I haven't heard from him. Why he hasn't texted me about what we should do for dinner tonight. Which just shows how crazy your brain can get after a loss.

How is it possible to forget for even a moment? Each morning when I wake up, I am amazed that I was able to sleep, even if only for four hours. I am amazed to wake up at all when I've cried myself to sleep until my chest hurts and I can't breathe. Yet here I am each day, awake. Breathing. Forced to trudge through another day. This week was especially tough, but for different reasons.

Tuesday night was Widows group. We're nearing the end of our time together, which ironically, causes both relief and fear to wash over me. As hard as each session is, I've grown accustomed to spending time with these diverse, wonderful women. It's almost as though we've come to lean on each other. None of us is exactly sure what we're getting from these meetings but judging by the expressions on their faces— and mine— we aren't ready for our group to end yet.

Half the time I drive home crying because we've just spent two hours churning up thoughts and emotions that normal people try to avoid. But our group leader, a determined septuagenarian psychologist lovingly pries us open each week, in the effort to prod us forward in our journey, her intent being to make us more prepared and accepting of moving forward in our lives.

I think we've gotten used to being naked in front of each other, because most of us are panicking over the thought of it ending. So, we're working together to keep it going in some form after our final session next week. Anyway, Tuesday night was bad enough. We all had to read the letters we'd written to our spouses. By the time our session ended, I had a massive crying headache. I drove home, intent on falling into bed as soon as I arrived. Instead, on the front porch was a large box, waiting to be lugged inside. Assuming it was something I'd ordered for the girls for Christmas, I dragged it in. I was so exhausted I debated leaving it for the next day. But this one was so heavy and oddly shaped I decided to go ahead and open it.

Instead of presents for the girls, I discovered a beautiful, live, miniature Christmas tree in a wooden planter. There was another small box of twinkle lights and ornaments to decorate it. After half an hour of breaking down the box and watering the tree, I found the receipt in the bottom of the box. My gift was from all the women at work. I burst into tears all over again.

How is it possible? These kind, beautiful women and their unbelievable thoughtfulness. On a terrible night when all I could think driving home was of what I've lost this year, and these wonderful women prove me wrong. To be thinking of me—eight months later. To still be watching out for me. To realize that underneath our day to day, surface interactions, they all know I still desperately need their care.

At a time of year when everyone is so busy getting ready for the holidays, these amazing women were thinking of me. I am so humbled by their extraordinary kindness. The next day, a gorgeous wreath arrived, a companion for the front door. So, despite my appalling lack of holiday spirit, their thoughtfulness spurred me into tossing the squishy pumpkin that had started leaking on the dining table. I put on a winter tablecloth, and I have my beautiful tree sitting in the middle of the table. Ginger likes it, too. She never climbs on the table, but she's been up there to sniff it a few times since. I've added a candle that I'll try to remember to light when I'm here at night. For what started out as an incredibly sad week, it sure has ended on a much better note.

Each night driving home from work, I pass the church on the corner. On the message board this week, the illuminated message says *There is still light in the darkness.* Is that Dan sending me a message? Because this year has been pretty friggin' dark. But we continue slogging to the finish line on what I can only pray will be the worst year of my life.

I don't know how I'll feel on New Year's Eve. Aside from sadness, will there be some sense of relief? That we've made it? It's not as though next year will magically be better. I can admit that now. Yet, part of me is seriously hoping it will get incrementally easier. Even if it's just a marginal improvement. Just slightly more bearable? It's not like I'll ever get over Dan's death. But it would be nice if I could spend less time crying over what we've lost and maybe start being grateful for getting to have him for as long as I did. I'm certainly not there yet. But it's what I hope for. We'll see what happens.

Iris update: basically, I have nothing new to report. She still won't come out from under the bed when I visit her. Every morning before work and every night when I get home, I try to spend a good twenty minutes in her room. Even though she won't come out, I talk to her anyway. Since Ginger still takes no real interest in the closed door, I've decided it would be best to keep them apart for the next several weeks. No sense stressing Iris even more than she already is. By the time I feed Iris and sit on the floor talking to her, Ginger is usually waiting for me outside the door. She starts poking her paw under the door when she thinks I've been talking long enough.

When I'm in there with Iris, sitting cross-legged on the floor, I find I have lots to chat about with her. Sometimes I hear a soft mew in response. I know she's listening. Trying to pick up clues about this strangely quiet sixth house she finds herself in. She's obviously traumatized by being moved so much. By losing her home. By being bullied by other cats along the way. Everything she knew has blown apart. In her own way, cowering under the bed, she's doing her best to adjust. Sort of like me. For now, she's eating well. And she's using the litter box. So, all things factored in—not too shabby. Things could definitely be worse.

# # #

9 months: 'Celebrating' Christmas. Everyone can relate to the expression "misery loves company". We've all known someone who seems to fit that description. However, I'd like to start a trend for an updated version of what may have been a misunderstanding all along. On behalf of the newly miserable, I'd like to suggest a tweak. How about "Grief appreciates understanding". Grief loves—not company, certainly, but compassion. For those of us who have experienced this life-altering state, we would never wish to inflict this abyss of pain on any other human being. Enemy or otherwise. Perhaps all the miserable people out there are simply worn down. Perhaps they're tired or in pain or they've lost all their joy. Maybe they never had it to begin with; or maybe they were exquisitely happy until their joy received several blows to the face. Until they, too were hit by the pain of an all-encompassing loss.

If anyone had ever told me I would spend nine months of this year (so far) crying over my husband's sudden death, I obviously wouldn't have wanted to believe them. In the small, dark, terrified corner of our hearts, we acknowledge that "the worst" *could* happen. Yet, we keep that fear stuffed away in the back of the closet. Safely hidden from ourselves and others; always praying the "worst" is so damn far down the road that we are completely safe to be happy now. We hope that "if" we have to deal with it later (not when), we'll somehow be magically more prepared for it. Or we will have had so much happy, loving time together that we'll be more "ready". Or accepting. Or stronger.

Trust me, we won't. We all know the day is coming, but when that chair is wrenched out from under you; the fall is still going to end with you breaking your ass when you hit the floor. It's still going to end with you, writhing in pain. With you not only wondering 'will I ever walk again' . . . but 'can I even get up off the damn floor'?

Christmas has finally passed. And we survived it. Like a great, looming storm cloud, it has hovered over the horizon for the past month, making me nervous about the damage it could inflict. Making me wish for its safe passing. I could finally move beyond such a significant landmark. In my best years, which frankly never seemed all that great before, Christmas was weighted with stress over the deadlines. The cleaning. The decorating. The wrapping. The cooking. The rampage of frivolous spending. The pressure to get it all done by the 25th.

I was wrong, of course. With the benefit of hindsight, those years truly *were* the best. Because Dan was still here with me to commiserate. To complain with. To divide and conquer on all the holiday tasks. To run to 7 Eleven for those last-minute holiday scratchers I love to put in the girls' stockings, but I always end up forgetting to buy. Dan wouldn't even blink when I asked him to pick up fifty. At that point, we were already numb to spending money. What was another fifty? Because there were always extra people to buy for. Friends of the girls', stopping by for a fun evening. Last year, a boyfriend. Our last Christmas together was probably our best. We'd shared a wonderful day with the girls and the first boyfriend—who will likely become our son-in-law if everything goes according to destiny. Boyfriend Two couldn't make it, but we'd sent him presents and a stocking with holiday scratchers, too.

Last Christmas, we didn't know it would be our last together. After thirty-six spent together, Dan would be gone only three months later. I will be forever grateful that we enjoyed the hell out of it. It was as close to perfection as we'll ever likely see again. Or at least until a few grandchildren come along to provide the unbridled joy and enthusiasm I now long to see again.

Dan was always like a kid at Christmas. Even though he hated all the shopping (the *single* day he crammed literally everyone on his list in a whirlwind shopping trip was enough to make him complain), he loved watching the girls open the gifts he'd picked out for them. He took pride in wrapping everything himself. Dan was a hard man to buy for because he was so No Frills. He didn't like anyone "wasting" money on clothes for him.

He never wore a watch (or even his wedding ring). Because of his propensity for losing it, I'd taken away his wedding band about three months after our honeymoon. He'd tried to wear it. Wanted to wear it. But the metal band was as unfamiliar on his finger as a winter coat (which he also wouldn't wear). After losing it in the surf on Diamond Head on our honeymoon, he proceeded to lose it a few more times after we returned. Finally, after finding it rolling around in the laundry basket, I just took it away from him. It's still buried in my jewelry box, waiting for the day one of our girls might want it as a keepsake.

Christmas gifts for Dan were slim pickings among obvious choices. His hobbies were sports. Each year, the girls would get creative with minor league baseball jerseys from different, far-flung teams. Books on baseball or football. Tickets to future Nationals games they could attend together. Popover mixes for him to continue mastering his quest for the perfect popover. And chocolate covered cherries. He loved them. Chelsea does, too. Half the time, it was a competition to see who could eat more on Christmas morning before somebody started feeling like they were going to barf.

This year, no one bought cherries. Just seeing them in the store was enough to get my heart pounding and my throat closing up. I would suddenly be fighting back tears. This year, none of the supposedly important tasks even got done. No decorating. No tree. No lights outside. Presents for the girls and boyfriends and the packages I had to ship. Believe me, the lack of stress over Christmas this year was so much worse than the years I felt overwhelmed. I would've rather been complaining— about a million little tasks that needed doing, if it meant I could've been doing them with Dan.

This year we treated Christmas as something to run away from. Like Thanksgiving, the girls didn't want to return home to a place so filled with happy memories. So, we devised an escape plan. A mini vacation to a festive place we hoped would be cheery enough to seep inside us, filling us with some level of spirit, no matter how dark we actually felt. Our goal—just get through the holiday. Together. United in our sadness yet hoping for a glimmer of fun that would tell us we would make it through the days. If not unscathed, then at least not suicidal. Each of us was hyper aware of what this overblown holiday represented. The biggest of the 'first' holidays. The one most fraught with hyped up visions of what it was supposed to be.

Despite each of us having moments when we crumpled, we did it together. We held each other up. At the end of Christmas day, we exhaled a collective sigh of relief. The next day would be *just Wednesday*. A typical day we could pretend was 'normal'. I'm calling it an official win for team Giordano. I believe we were successful. In keeping it simple, we were relieved and happy to be together. Boyfriend Two gets a huge assist for driving nearly four hours on Christmas Eve to be with us. His thought was that if he were there, maybe it wouldn't feel so glaringly obvious that Dan was missing. That we were so markedly "only three". Boyfriend Two now holds a special place in my heart forever.

After a long drive in the opposite direction from his own family, he joined us for Christmas Eve dinner and spent the night in our hotel suite. After breakfast and presents together, he hopped in his car and drove nearly four hours back to his parents, in time to catch their afternoon celebration. I will always be grateful to him for his incredible thoughtfulness. Like a pressure cooker relieving steam, I felt myself relaxing a bit more as soon as he arrived. Boyfriend Two is equally as special as Boyfriend One. He is kind and thoughtful and funny and so very good for my daughter. I appreciate him more than you can imagine. If the Boyfriends have made this year even one percent easier for our girls to endure, they forever have my undying love and devotion. With their loving compassion, they have done wonders helping my girls navigate this awful year.

Unfortunately, we now have a much better idea what it's like to miss someone desperately. To have a hole inside us too large to fill. Maybe ever. We had moments of fun and merriment, still grateful we are able to laugh and love and be loved. And we had moments of aching sadness. Nine months in, there are still moments of disbelief that we have been transported to this strange, foreign land we will never be able to leave. Most importantly, at least this first year, is the fact that we got through it. We *survived* Christmas. For this year, surviving has to be enough.

# # #

Hindsight: As I wrote this book, my working title was *The Runaway Years*. Especially at the holidays, I felt if I could just run away, I might possibly feel better. I might possibly forget my loss for even a brief period each day. However, we all know that doesn't work. I could have spent a year in Hawaii after Dan died and it still would have been the worst year of my life. There is no running away from grief and pain and sadness.

After the loss of your spouse, holidays will suck. Not forever, I hope. But for a long while. They also require an adjustment to our expectations. The traditions will never be what they were to us before. So, isn't it better (in my opinion) to maybe go for something different? Nothing can compare to what you lost. So, why try?

My holidays that first year (and the couple since) have been different, not only because my husband is gone, but because we are forever changed by the loss. If I could offer any recommendations, it would be to be very gentle with yourself. If you don't want to decorate, if you don't want to wrap gifts, if you don't want to cook big meals. Whatever it is you are having trouble facing, then don't do it. Change it up for one year. Try something crazy or different. Something where there are no expectations other than surviving it. Maybe the change becomes permanent. Or maybe you'll find that next year, you'd like to bring back a few of your traditions. You don't have to force yourself to do the things you have always done.

On the flip side, if traditions bring you a level of comfort, then of course, you should do them. The point I make here is to do what *you* want. Do whatever it takes to get through them. That first year for us was travel. Running away from our memories. That's what worked for us in year one. Making the unbearable slightly more bearable.

Questions to contemplate: What do I want? What do my kids need? What will make it easier for me to get through this particular day? What does everyone around me want? Note to self: You don't care as much about that last one. Think about what is important to you. What is easier for you? What will help you get through this day? You. You. You. See—it's a full sentence.

Iris update: It's been four weeks now. Between the Thanksgiving and Christmas trips, I've been away for eight of those days. But tonight, Iris poked her head out from under the bed and stared at me when I brought dinner and fresh water to her room. She has a tiny smudge of orange on her forehead! I think I can confirm she is actually a tortie, not that I've seen any of the rest of her yet. Just her head. I sat on the floor for the next ten minutes trying to coax her out. But she's not ready to leave her safe space yet. But she chirped at me when I talked to her. Progress! Ginger is still oblivious to her. It's not as though Iris is a viable threat to Ginger's total domination of the house.

# # #

New Year's 2018: It's finally a new year. My kind-hearted neighbors took pity on me and invited me out New Year's Eve to get Chinese food. Their suggestion startled me at first. That's what Dan and I would always do. Chinese takeout or barbecue for our New Year's Eve spent at home. We'd eat in the living room and flip between the network shows to catch as many acts as possible. My neighbors are a little older, so we went out to dinner at six. I was home and in my jammies by eight. And I watched all the shows by myself. Drank a little. Not champagne. It didn't really feel like a celebration of anything, except maybe survival. I ended up going to bed at ten-thirty.

New Year's Day doesn't feel any different. Though the pessimist in me expected this, part of me held out hope the first day of a fresh, clean year would feel magically better. I'd hoped that leaving the worst year of my life in the dark void as the clock struck midnight would be more than just symbolic. But, as I sit here watching the Rose Parade, I don't feel any different. Still sort of weepy. Still alone. Still trying to plod along as though I've adjusted to my new normal. Truthfully, if there's been any adjustment, it's still involuntary.

As I evaluate my status at the nine-months-and-change point I can acknowledge I cry a little less. Four times a week, down from seven. I smile more frequently. My sleep has improved slightly. I've gotten more skilled at keeping busy. I experience less panic as the weekend approaches. New Year's was a test of that. Four days off with nowhere to run away to. But I persevered. I'm on day four, grateful I can return to work tomorrow, although the past three days weren't entirely bad. I kept busy with chores, both manufactured and legit. A couple times I found myself surprised the day had eroded faster than expected.

Hopefully, this year will bring much needed peace. A softened version of grief. I will hope for happiness but am resigned to continued sadness. It's a little too much to ask for happy after losing the person who made you that way for thirty-six years. I find I'm becoming more comfortable with sadness. The time we had together was truly worth a few years of sadness. Selfishly, I hope this year for a few moments of joy mixed in. Maybe a couple signs that he's happy where he is now. That would truly make this year more bearable for me. Not sure Dan can deliver on that wish, but I'll be looking for signs.

# # #

9.5 months: Finding Peace in a Baking Show. I have finally discovered a way to achieve a nearly Zen like state where grief goes away for brief periods of time. If it wasn't true (for me, anyway) it would likely be funny. My miracle? The Great British Baking Show. I highly recommend you give it a try. Though I'd heard of it, I first discovered the show last spring.

Shortly after Dan died, I was floundering every evening wondering how to fill the time after work. The hours between arriving home to an empty house and the time I could finally attempt to go to bed. Most nights I would exhaust myself walking with my beloved neighbor, whose calm and spiritual outlook on life served to smooth my ragged edges in the darkest early days. I will forever be beholden to her for her kindness in taking me on. But I digress.

On Fridays especially, I tended to feel more overwhelmed than usual as I faced the daunting task of an entire weekend of time to fill. One evening, about a month after Dan died, I was searching through endless cable channels in a quest to find something distracting. I tuned in to PBS and discovered the Great British Baking Show. And experienced the first moment of peace. If you've never seen it, it is a show based in Britain featuring a dozen or so amateur bakers on their quest to be named best home baker in Britain.

Lots of scenery shots of bleating sheep and goats; lots of drifting bumblebees hovering over beautiful country gardens drifting with lavender. You can almost smell the wafting scent if you close your eyes. But don't close your eyes because you'll miss the delightful scenery. The prize at the end of the season is a rather nondescript glass cake stand that all of the bakers, a diverse cast of young, old, black, white, Indian, Asian, Hispanic, male and female are striving to achieve.

The hosts all have drool-worthy British accents, (they pronounce oregano as "oregaahno"). How can you not love it? The judges are stern with their criticism, yet gentle in how they dispense it. Paul Hollywood is the sexy yet demanding judge. Mary Berry (the early seasons) and later, Prue Leith are grandmotherly, yet sometimes devious in their challenges, Mary whisks the bakers into a frenzy before declaring their masterpiece to be "scrummy". The bakers sweat with terror over the possibility they might overbake their creations, or worse—be guilty of a "soggy bottom". Who hasn't suffered that shame? Judge Paul can make the contestants crumble with just a stare. Did you notice what I did there—*"crumble"* on a baking show? Funny, right? Okay, I'll just get back to my point.

On GBBS, the judges' constructive comments are founded in their desire for perfection, yet unlike so many shows here in the US, the judges' comments are tempered by kindness and understanding that they hold each baker's sponge cake heart in their hands. Each week, the bakers are tested by three difficult challenges before one person is eliminated. Each week, the person being eliminated is left desolate, along with all the contestants who have befriended him. There is not a moment of cruelty or competition or backstabbing during this glorious hour. I am left both riveted by the show and confused by how different the British are from us. It also brings up several questions for me about British baking in general: what is treacle? What is a bap? A toad in the hole?? Is a soggy bottom truly the curse they all believe it is? Is a "pudding" better than dessert? Does it *mean* dessert? Why does a 'tray bake' sound more promising than what we would likely view as a pan of glammed up brownies?

Surprisingly, this show doesn't make me want to bake, nor eat most of these recipes I've never heard of. Except maybe Mary Berry's famous cherry cake, which sounds more lemony and delightful than cherry. When she says the cake is 'scrummy', I completely believe her. Watching GBBS leaves me in a state of restful peace as I absorb the adorable accents; the snippets of British countryside; the playful jokes offered as the contestants sweat out another challenge.

At no time during that brief hour each Friday night did I think of Dan. Of all that I'd lost. Of my now shattered life. I just focused with an almost abnormal clarity on that week's challenge. On the perfect biscuits (cookies); the disasters that lie in wait as you temper chocolate; the shame of an over-proofed dough. The delight of a properly made butter cream. I find myself googling 'what are sultanas?' FYI, sultanas are whizzled, white grapes.

Digression from my story: Okay, so I know that *whizzled* isn't actually a word, but really—shouldn't it be? It is far more descriptive that 'wizened'. Wizened is just boring. It even looks boring written out. Over the years, my girls and I have created several words that we use with relative abandon. It's only when someone questions the word that we remember we made it up. We also created 'jamitize'. Use it in a sentence, you ask? I'll set the scene . . . it's bedtime, so I would say, "hey, girls, it's time to brush your teeth and jamitize so we can get in bed for story time." I'll let you be the judge of our creative use of the English language.

Okay – so back to GBBS. Nearly ten months into this dreaded new normal, the Great British Baking Show has been my tiny miracle this year. My quiet in the storm. The soothing balm to calm my restless mind when real life frequently becomes too overwhelming to bear. If you've never seen it, I highly recommend it.

Once I became addicted to GBBS, I had to go back and watch every season. Then, I followed up with their holiday specials. And then, the master classes where Paul and Mary do the baking, showing us where the contestants erred during the regular season. And then I get to start them all over again while I wait for new seasons. On weekends when I can't fill the endless hours with chores and errands, I can binge watch a comforting and familiar friend. As crazy as it sounds, I am so grateful to have found something pleasant to distract my mind when real life gets to be too much. I now contemplate a day when I might actually be up for the challenge of Grandmother Berry's magnificent cherry cake.

# # #

Hindsight: There is something out there that will soothe your mind. I guarantee it. If only to offer you an hour's respite from the nightmare our lives have become. For me, it used to be reading. I could lose myself in a book for several hours to relieve the stress of the day or a tough week. But, in that first year after Dan, I was too distracted to make it through even a chapter. I kept praying for my concentration to return, yet it didn't. It took me closer to two years before I could finally get lost in a book again. That's a long time to go without comfort. I will always hold a fond place in my heart for GBBS because it was like a cherished blanket I could snuggle into and forget my life for an hour or two.

Last year, I tried paint-by-number and that worked for me, too. Believe me, paint by number has come a long way from the creepy, scary clown pictures of my youth. You can still find a psychedelic cat if that's what you're into, but there are some pretty nice florals, landscapes, etc. you can try instead. The important thing is that you have to concentrate on what you are doing, which means you can't be dwelling on your situation. Another suggestion: jigsaw puzzles. Or baking. Reading. Knitting. Model building. Something that requires total absorption. Maybe writing? The key is something you have to focus on, but not something so challenging that it becomes just one more frustration in your life.

Seriously consider busting out the card table and just leaving it up in your living room. When the stress starts crashing down, pick up that paint brush or go back to the puzzle and spread it out on the table. I guarantee you'll get caught up in it for at least an hour, and for me, it's more likely to be two or three hours. You can get puzzles and paint by number kits on many sites, but they're plentiful and cheap on Amazon.

I was wrapping up this book during the pandemic, so the games idea is one you've likely already hit on if you've been trapped inside for the last twelve months. But, grief is very different from boredom. Activities will help fill the time in both situations, but for me, losing myself in an activity was vital in helping me shut off my brain for brief periods of time. Long enough to sometimes regain my balance during the grief process. Everyone needs a respite from their grief. If only for a few hours. Allow yourself to find something that will help you shut your brain off. You deserve a rest.

Iris update: Iris emerged from under the bed one night this week as I sat quietly on the floor. I held my breath. She didn't come close. She just stared at me for several minutes. Then she walked over to her food bowl and ate her Sheba. She even turned her back on me to eat while I sat there, so I'm counting that as a success. A smidgen of trust? Or just super hungry? I'll report back later.

# # #

10 months: **Resilience**. I forgot the date this week. The 28th came and went without me recognizing it was the ten-month mile marker of Dan being gone. I remembered on the 31st that I'd missed it. But it seems as though I've been running behind all month. Today feels like it should only be the middle of the month. Not that I'm sad about time passing faster. Though I am now able to acknowledge that my growing suspicions about the one-year mark are likely correct. The official one year will not bring much relief from missing my husband—but it'll still be an important milestone for me. For the girls.

It will be a marker that we survived this year of awfulness. That I'm still standing. That I'm still strong. At this point, I am a beast. My body and soul imploded that night. I have endured every terrible night and day since. Despite feeling as though a big part of me died that night, too, it's remarkable to me to discover there's still something left of me. Some small kernel of determination and fury and resentment that refuses to die. Refuses to allow Dan's death to destroy me or our girls.

I don't know if that's something to be proud of? Perhaps surprised by? I've hated hearing over and over that I'm strong. That I'm holding up so well. That we're going to be fine. That we're going to make it. Do we have a choice? Before Dan's death I would've said I didn't want to make it. It's like that joke about dieting. Take away all the sugar and fat and fun and you'll live longer— or it'll just *feel* longer.

The jury's still out on whether I actually want to be here. My life now is a salad. A healthy, lonely, boring salad. Nutritious, but not what I really want. I want the oozing jelly donut again. I want the greasy pizza. I lost the sweet. I lost the zest. The fun. The laughter. The joy of a single person knowing you better than you know yourself. The unconditional love of the only person who's had my back since I was eighteen. I lost the best part of me. Do I really want the next thirty years to feel like fifty?

My history with Dan began when I was eighteen and he was twenty. A blind date. To give you an idea of his personality, that first night we were stopped by the cops on the way home. Dan walked away from it without a ticket. He was polite and charming to the cop who stopped us for a missing taillight. From that night on, we became inseparable. What most people don't know is how much normalcy and stability Dan brought to my world. My life until that point had been at best, unpleasant. My parents were selfish narcissists who despised each other yet were inexplicably tied together—destined to make each other miserable for more than fifty years before my father finally died.

My father was a lazy, bullying tyrant. As a teacher, I believe he was well-liked—at least by his students. He was easygoing (outside of our home) and an easy "A" for his students. At home, he was a brooding, moody monster. My brothers and I learned at a very young age to keep out of his way. Avoidance was the solution to growing up in a cluttered, depressing home with parents who fought constantly. My mother was only marginally better at parenting. Abandoned by her own mother when she was eight, Mom was content to play doormat and victim to my father's overbearing, argumentative nature. He was a gas lighter and a cheater, basically from the start of their marriage. It was his operating philosophy. If there was an opportunity to skirt the system, he was first in line to take advantage. For my mother, it was easier to endure his repulsive behavior and complain bitterly than it would have been to just leave him.

Leaving would have required her to get a job to support herself, something she absolutely refused to do. Working was for 'other women'. She liked her soap operas. She liked pretending she was in a successful marriage. A dozen bracelets on her arm meant we were rich. And she was *happy*. Her decade-old Cadillac offered the illusion of wealth—when the car was actually running. She could overlook the shabby, falling-down-around-us dump we lived in. It was more important to pretend. That her husband wasn't a cruel bastard. That she'd chosen well because she was 'taken care of'. To this day, my mother likes to believe she *never* had a choice. But, to eleven-year-old me who had to endure her daily litany of his faults and transgressions, watching the daily drama of cruelty, disrespect and rage—I always believed that picking *easy* over *difficult* was a choice. Choosing to stay over leaving him *was* a choice. Deciding not to act—was a choice.

My father, the sometimes high, sometimes drunk, but always disengaged parent could be old-fashioned when it was convenient for him. At various points in our lives, he made idiotic decisions we all had to endure. Did I really need medicine for my asthma attacks? He'd read somewhere that drinking lots of coffee would work just as well. I ended up in the hospital for a week that time. He believed we were all "safer" once he removed all the locks from our bedroom doors "in case we locked ourselves in". He actually went around and gutted all the locks so there was virtually no way any of us could have privacy in our bedrooms or even in the bathroom.

At one point, he decided my brothers and I could only wash our hair once a week—to save water. The same man who would empty the pool each year and refill it with fresh water—instead of covering it in the fall like normal people did—and shocking it with chemicals in the spring. Luckily, he also had the tendency to disappear for days at a time, so the hair-washing issue was something we could all sneak in while he was AWOL. Imagine the pressure of a high school girl—having to *sneak* around to wash her hair. Most kids worry about getting caught drinking. I worried whether I could get a shower without someone walking in on me.

Later, when I was fifteen, Dad arbitrarily decided I couldn't date guys my age because "he knew what guys that age were after". If I wanted to date, he would arrange for me to date his friends. His *forty-five-year-old* poker buddies—who would "treat me right". My father ran a poker game in our basement three nights a week. That meant there were various oddities of human existence perpetually wandering in and out of our house at all hours of the day and night. One of his derelict friends had clearly spotted me.

My heart is pounding as I write this—forty years later. As I relive that awful time in my life. Afraid to go home, for fear of what my father would think of next to torture us all. At some point, Dad decided I would go out on a date with one of his poker buddies—because the friend *had expressed an interest in me*. Read that again. His friend—the pervy pedophile—had noticed me. In my home with doors that didn't lock. And he'd asked my father whether he could date me. My father-of-the-year thought this was a *good* idea. Back in those days, no one talked about pedophiles. We apparently just endured them.

This *great guy*—who I later discovered was a high school teacher in a neighboring town, had expressed interest in me. At age fifteen, I stood there, paralyzed with terror as I tried to explain to my father why I didn't want to go out with his pervy friend. That I'd rather date *no one* than go out with a gross, old guy. My complaint, of course, fell on deaf ears. In fact, it only served to piss him off. That I would dare question his authority. My two younger brothers (14 and 11) tried to defend me. My mother, to my everlasting disgust, finally suggested "for chrissakes, just go out with him-" Yes—her answer was to "get it over with" so my father would stop ranting. I look back as an adult and try to accept the fact that she was just as trapped as the rest of us. But it's still a hard sell for me. Once you have kids of your own and you know what you would do for them- My mother's inaction is still hard to make excuses for when I think about what we endured.

Growing up in that house, I'd realized at a pretty young age that I was on my own. I was always hyper aware that I needed to take care of myself. That I needed to stay ever vigilant. Sad, isn't it? That I have specific memories of feeling dangerously alone. At age 8. 9. 10? By eleven, I knew I had to protect myself. That there was literally no one—not my weakened, downtrodden mother, not a neighbor, not a stranger who would be there to fight for me. By age eleven, I was mentally a forty-year-old, trapped in the body of a child. I knew the only way I'd make it out would be to get good grades and get the hell away from them. That if I screwed up in any way, I'd be done for. Like prey. If I stumbled, I'd be dragged back into the bowels of the cave, never to be seen again.

That day, at age fifteen, standing in the kitchen, my heart in my throat as I watched every potential avenue of escape close off, I mentally prepared myself to run away from home. Where would I go? Who would take me in? How would I get to school? As my father began explaining that the pedophile would be taking me out for a nice dinner, etc., my mind was working feverishly to find a way to save myself.

Out of nowhere—I blurted out that if I was made to go on the date, I would call Child Protective Services and report him. My father, a half-assed, lazy teacher himself (with a job to protect); and the pedophile—another high school teacher (with a job and likely a stable full of potential future victims to groom) and my mother—the worn-out caricature of a parental figure. (Not that I said it that way, but you get the drift). Time stood still as my father's mouth dropped open. I waited for him to deck me. His methods of control were raging at us and hitting us.

But somehow, my words sunk into that thick skull. In a matter of moments—the situation unraveled. Not apologizing in any way, my father backed down. His words? "Forget it. I was trying to help you—but if you'd rather be an ungrateful bitch, then just forget it."

For months after, I slept with one eye open, my baseball bat hidden under the bed, the grip directly under the head of the bed, where I could reach it. I hoped. I practiced snatching it from a prone position. My mind played out scenarios – if I were asleep, would I remember it was there? Could I reach it from both sides of my twin bed? Did I need to borrow my brother's bat, too? Remember—we had no locks on our doors—and drunken, drugged poker-playing riffraff wandering through our five-room tenement at all hours of the night.

My father's *friends* seemed to have free range at our house. Like most things, my mother didn't fight back over the unreasonableness of my dad holding poker games in the basement. Over middle-aged guys getting high in our basement as she tried to raise three kids. Their being allowed to sleep off a drunk in my brothers' and my bedrooms. We'd arrive home from school in the afternoon to a cigarette and vodka hazed stench emanating from our bedrooms. Strangers lying *between* our sheets, sleeping off their poker losses. Where to do homework? No one seemed to care. There was no escape in the tiny ranch. In good weather, I'd take my homework outside to the rotting picnic table. In bad weather, we'd be forced to do our work in the cluttered kitchen, hoping no one noticed us sitting at the table. Praying the strangers in our beds would get up and leave before it was time for us to go to bed ourselves.

To describe Dan as a godsend to my life is pretty much understating it. He was the first person I'd ever known who cared more about me than I did. He cared enough for ten people, softening the hardened nugget that my heart was becoming. After years of casual cruelty and emotional siege, Dan was the person who finally made me whole. He loved me—just the way I was. Unconditionally. He protected me from my father. He intervened when my mother's manipulative edge would start to overwhelm me. He had unwavering faith in me. In us.

I'm so grateful I was only eighteen when I met him. Because without him, I would have shaped into a completely different person. I would have been cynical. Bitter about men. Gun-shy about relationships. As good as Dan was, it took years to overcome the damage my parents inflicted. The lack of trust I had. The fierce self-reliance I'd learned to depend on. The belief that Dan couldn't possibly be as good as he seemed. That it would all come crashing down eventually. But it never did. I'm so grateful I had thirty-six years with him. And I thanked God for him every single day after we met.

So now, ten months after his death . . . yeah— I've survived. I've made it this far. I can probably continue "making it". Part of me didn't want that to be true. As destroyed as I am on the inside; there's some damned resilience in me that has kept my outer shell intact. The toughness I had to learn at age eleven has returned full force. Perhaps it never left me. It was able to lie dormant through all the Dan years when his love was my force field, resting up for the day it would be called back into action.

How do I feel now? Battle worn, numb, fatigued. How I imagine it must feel after a long, unrelenting war. Or a magnitude 8 earthquake, where you survive to walk among rubble every day. The world you knew no longer exists. The place you now live is a wasteland; the people who matter most to you are all gone; yet among the ruins, you somehow remain standing. You still exist—for an unknown purpose. Struggling to survive. Scrounging for food and water and shelter in a war-torn land. All signs suggest you should just give up. Let go. Quietly slip away. Yet, we don't. We're stupidly determined. We're scrappy. We don't quit. Just as a mutant seed will fight to find the soil and water and light. As it fights to regenerate after destruction. As my shattered heart slowly begins to repair itself, I've been able to hold it together for everyone else. And I'm finally realizing— I'm holding it together for me too. While part of me is grateful for this steely resilience, another part of me really wants to punch Resilience in the face.

Resilience forces you to choose. To exist. To endure. To go on. To hang out here until it's my time to join Dan again. To remain in a barren wasteland where I'll have to voluntarily seek each scrap of joy—none of them including him. As I read this back, I sound pretty pathetic but at this point, I'm struggling to find the significance to my life as it stands now. What am I here for? Aside from seeing it through with the girls, what am I supposed to do with all this time? Fill it with friends and travel and learning to knit? Plays? Concerts? While all of that will be pleasant and enjoyable, it just sounds so hollow. I guess it's because I'm viewing pleasure and leisure as a trade-off for losing Dan. Which isn't entirely true. If things had gone the way they were supposed to, Dan and I would have enjoyed those things together.

Am I supposed to sit on the couch, watching endless hours of Netflix? Wallow alone and live half a life? Work until I drop? Even writing that sounds pathetic. Write more books? I'm trying to return to writing. I try to lay out all the stories in my head, but the longer I'm away from it, the harder it becomes to return to the hard work of writing. Is my writing just one *more* thing I loved that I will also lose? The business of writing is very time-consuming (a good thing), but it's also very isolating (a bad thing), now that I am already alone so much. Is it healthy to spend more time alone? Or do I give up writing until I regain a sense of balance?

What am I really meant to do? I wish I had Dan's perspective on this. He was always able to cut through all the noise and remind me what was important. I hate losing his insight. If he can see me writing this, maybe he can send me a sign. I'd appreciate it.

# # #

10 months and change: Sports & Predictions Dan's Patriots won the Super Bowl last week. I didn't experience any joy, except for Chelsea winning the 3rd and 4th quarters in my office Super Bowl pool. A special shout out to Dan for the gust of wind that blew the Rams' field goal attempt to the left. Throughout their season, I took it as gospel the Pats would win it all. Just like there was never a doubt about the Red Sox last fall; I knew Dan's teams would win. It was just his year. Whether the wins were to make up for him having to leave us, or maybe he simply had a hand in it, I knew the outcomes long before the games were ever played. Maybe it was Dan's way of showing us that things are pretty damned good up there. Maybe heaven for him is the joy of his team playing each day under a perfect sky and every game ends with victory.

Although writing about this makes me cry, I have a tiny sliver of peace. Watching the Super Bowl, knowing Dan was helping his team win. Maybe next year I'll be able to smile when I think about him watching sports. Ten months in, I still catch myself glancing to his leather chair expecting to see him there, leaning forward, intent on the next play; but still eager to explain a play to me, even if he'd already explained it a dozen times before.

In any case, I'm already planning for his divine intervention during March Madness. Dan's team was Virginia. Like the Sox and Patriots, I'm making the prediction that the Wahoos will go all the way during March Madness *this* year. They were expected to go all the way last year. Ranked number one, coached by the incredibly steadfast and cool-under-pressure Tony Bennett. The Cavaliers were unbeatable throughout the season. They were a shoo-in to win it all. And everyone's brackets reflected that. Last year, UVA was ranked first, yet, in a colossal choke, they were eliminated in the first round—in humiliating fashion by a team ranked 16th. Millions of brackets—busted on the first day. Since no one will be eager to embrace UVA again this year, I will stealthily pick them to go all the way, knowing that Dan will have a hand in it.

When UVA lost last March, Dan was heartbroken. It was only weeks later that he would die—at a UVA baseball game, hosted by VCU. He loved Virginia. He would travel to Charlottesville with his sports buddy M for baseball, football and basketball games. Our girls both graduated from UVA. Dan still held a soft spot for VCU, too, since he worked there, and it gave him one more reason to buy season tickets. During the VCU Rams' golden run-up to the 2011 basketball Final Four, Dan was as excited as anyone else on campus. For an inner-city school no one had ever heard of, with no football team—it was a pretty amazing event to be a part of. The whole city rallied behind them. When VCU's bookstore was absolutely overrun with fans trying to buy merchandise, the administration put out a desperate call for volunteers willing to pitch in with the overflow crowds at the bookstore. Accountant Dan eagerly volunteered, so happy to be part of the excitement that was taking place.

He was like that about most things. Throwing himself into it full force. He coached our daughters' softball teams for nearly a decade, his buddy M at his side as they muddled through each season. Each lineup. His team was consistently terrible. The other coaches, each one more viciously competitive than the next, rigged the drafts so they could pluck the best kids for their own teams. Anyone with talent was stolen long before she hit the market.

In typical Dan fashion, he never cared that the deck was stacked against him. As spring approached, he would light up like a kid himself. So excited to coach another crop of girls— along with his daughters. Dan always inherited the girls who'd never played before.

The girls who were afraid of the ball. Girls who were more likely to run to third base than first. Girls who'd heard through the Terrible Player Grapevine that Dan would never, ever turn anyone away. The girls who'd heard he always packed a cooler of frozen treats for every practice and game. He was the guy who lugged around spare gloves and bats for the girls who had no equipment. His trunk was always packed with extra equipment he'd buy himself. Though his team was always consistently in last place, his team was also known throughout the league as the most fun. The year he was voted Coach of the Year, even the most viciously competitive coaches couldn't complain about it.

So much of what I miss now is the everyday stuff. The jokes. The lightheartedness. The "how was your day?" The easy back and forth chat about nothing. About where to get dinner on Thursday night. What sub to split for a quick supper. What plans would we make for the coming weekend? How we felt our retirement was shaping up. Shared worries or praise of our beautiful girls. Nothing earth shattering. Just the pleasant, easy buzz of conversation with the person you've spent 36 years with. Dan was always a big talker; far more than me.

Now, I come home to such overwhelming quiet. As I sit here waiting for this thousandth sad moment to pass, shoulders shaking, enduring what will likely be a dozen Kleenex cry, Ginger the cat is staring at me, worried by the strange sounds emanating from her sole caregiver. She strolls down the couch and plops into my lap for a few quick pets. I will view this as her comforting me, rather than the other way around. It feels slightly less awful if I can think of her as being here for me. In the absence of the husband I miss every minute of every day, at least I now have a Ginger. And if Iris would ever start trusting me, we could all be comforting each other. Every night would be girls' night. On the couch, watching Great British Baking

Show reruns—or Hallmark channel, with their happy, beautiful widows finding true love once again.

I hope tonight I'm able to sleep. Last night was a toss and turn night. It was freakishly warm for early February, and I lay awake most of the night not sleeping. Replaying Dan's face those last minutes he was alive. That expression I couldn't translate because it was so unfamiliar. Because I wasn't paying attention. A wistful sadness, as though he knew how bad it was. That it wasn't fixable. As though he'd already suspected what the outcome would be. And he chose to leave us before the final moment happened. Because he was afraid. For himself and maybe, as I think of it for the hundredth time, he was afraid for Chelsea and me. Or maybe he was just trying to outrun it. Walk it off. Pray and pretend it wasn't as bad as it turned out.

Anyway, that's the expression I see every night. The one I can't get out of my head. The one that reminds me continuously of my colossal failure. Will I ever be able to forgive myself? Would I actually feel any better if I could? Somehow, it doesn't seem as though forgiving myself will matter because the outcome can't ever change. It's not as though with forgiveness I could get him back. But maybe, I'd finally see a different Dan when I close my eyes. The funny, smiling face I saw ninety-nine percent of the time. Instead of his sad, worried eyes. If I could have one thing, I think I'd wish for that. And tonight especially, I'll pray that sleep will find me.

Iris update: It's been two months since Iris arrived. I go into her room every morning and every evening to feed her; scoop her litter and then I sit on the floor and talk to her. I can tell from the impression in the afghan I left on top of the bed that she has spent some time there, cuddled in the blanket. That makes me smile. She is at least starting to enjoy herself. I've also placed a chair by the window so she can look outside if she's so inclined.

As I sat cross-legged on the floor and talked to her under the bed, Iris poked her head out. I continued to chat, pretending I didn't notice as she slowly crept closer to me. Afraid to move, I reached out my hand, but the movement was too sudden for her. She darted back under the bed. After ten minutes of coaxing, she reappeared. This time, I kept my hand at my side. She approached cautiously, her wise, green eyes assessing for any sign of potential sinister activity on my part. She sniffed my sock. For the briefest second, she stepped over my crossed legs. Then she walked over to her bowl and ate her dinner. It was a good night.

# # #

Part Three

Comparison Is the Thief of Joy . . . Theodore Roosevelt

11 months: Two Steps Forward . . . I find I'm slightly less worried about dying too early and a little more interested in living—and living well. I'm finally accepting the fact that asking why Dan died only brings me to tears and still never provides me any answers. No answers I can accept. In some ways, I feel it might be better to finally stop asking. That's what I'm going to try anyway. I still cry often, but now when I do, it is less a drowning wave of sorrow. More often now, it is a moment when a memory overtakes me—and I realize that's all it will ever be again. My memories of us. What will happen when I start forgetting? When our memories fade, does the person fade with them?

I was in the car yesterday, driving north to meet Chelsea. I was excited. Eager to see her. The sky was blue after endless days of rain. I was . . . happy. Almost like I used to be—before. As I glanced at a streaky, purple cloud, a memory popped up out of nowhere. Dan and me. This drive. Together. Meeting Chelsea and her boyfriend for a quick Saturday night dinner.

With Chelsea living in DC, the traffic is unbearable. What should take ninety minutes can take anywhere from two and a half to three hours. North or south. Doesn't matter. At some point, Dan suggested we meet in the middle, so the drive wasn't bad for either of us. Quick dinners to check in with our eldest. To not be apart for too long. Any time there was going to be more than four or five weeks between visits, we would close the gap by meeting in the middle. Both of us driving halfway. The very thing I was doing at that moment. But today, I was alone. Talking to myself instead of chatting with Dan. And the tears just erupted.

One thing I've learned at this almost-a-year point is that I still can't predict how I will feel each day. Some days, it is still very much moment to moment. One minute I'm laughing over a joke at work. The next, I'm nearly doubled over with the wistful memory of something I no longer have. The sound of his voice sets me back in a way I could never have imagined. We have one brief clip of his voice, leaving a message for Chelsea; It was a typical Dan message. "Have a great day! I love you!" A week ago, Chelsea sent it to me. She plays it occasionally and it is a source of comfort to her. His voice in her ear. The way she'd always heard it over her twenty-eight years with him.

Dan was a glass-half-full guy. Nearly always happy, he was always enthusiastic. Grateful for the little things. The last day of his life, he was excited about the game that night. He had a habit of leaving us messages like that. I would listen, smile . . . and then delete them. If I had only known. It's unimaginable now, that out of the hundreds of messages he left us . . . only one remains—and we're hoarding it between the three of us.

When Chelsea sent me the voice clip, she didn't think to warn me first what it was. I played it, not knowing it was something I would need to be prepared for. There are so many things you miss about a person after they are gone. Everyone talks about missing their touch and their scent and their habits. But I hadn't a clue how much I missed his distinctive voice. He was such a talker. The life of the party. I always used to tease him that he spoke enough for three people. Hearing that happy, kid-like voice after 11 months of radio silence was like an electric current surging through my body. I sobbed like I had in the early days after he died. As though I would actually suffocate under the weight of my loss.

It's now a few weeks later and I haven't listened to it again. I'm not sure I can handle it. Yet, I can't possibly part with it. I'm so grateful to have it—yet the thought of hearing him again when I know I'll never see him again . . . makes me sick with loss. It's one of those things I'll have to revisit after more time passes. For now, I have no answers.

Hindsight: There will always be triggers that set off our grief and send us spiraling. We will likely never see most of them coming. A sound. A scent. A song. A dream we wake up crying from. And driving. What is it about driving? I have spent more time crying in my car since Dan died than I ever could have dreamed possible. It was like as soon as I was on the road, the tears just spontaneously erupted. I could be thinking about anything. Or nothing. On highways, on secondary roads. In the grocery store parking lot. In my driveway. In my parking space at work. Those first two years I was a danger to myself (and others) when I was in a car. I was weepy. I was distracted. I had Widow's Fog. Seriously. Be careful out there. Crying while driving is a Thing.

# # #

11 months and change: Glimpse of the Future? Something encouraging this month: The past few weeks I've started noticing the moments I am happy. That probably sounds odd to most people, but until Dan died, I'd never spent so long being so deeply depressed. Before Dan passed, I was a relatively normal person. Normal highs. Normal lows. Cranky bitch days wedged in occasionally, but my normal was pretty happy and low key.

Having felt so bad for so long, I've now begun noticing the things that make me feel good. Like when I go to the gym on a rainy, cold night after work. I still have to force myself to go. I'm not one of those dying-to-get-to-the-gym people. I'm still the maybe-

I'll-skip-it-just-this-once people. I'm actually more of a 'I'd rather go home and eat carbs' people. But, I force myself to go to the gym. Minimum three times a week, sometimes more. I'm tough on myself. Insulting. Bullying myself if I don't go. My reward is getting to watch an episode of GBBS Master Class. The comfort of Mary Berry's incredibly hard recipes and the charm of sexy Paul's accent as I walk another mile on the treadmill.

Something else that made me feel good recently. At work, I had to present a project to the board of directors a few weeks ago. Not a huge deal, but something I would've been nervous about last year. Now— I compare pretty much everything to the stress level of losing Dan, so there's obviously no comparison. Which has made me somewhat fearless about things I used to worry about. Sounds crazy, doesn't it? But, in a year when I've lost the most important thing in my life—I'm somehow still standing. So, what could there possibly be at work that could stress me out?

Still on the list of things that make me afraid: a mouse in the cabinet; a hornet in my house; finding a snake anywhere; a scary sound in the dead of night; an almost irrational fear of anything happening to the girls. So—even with my sudden bravery about work stuff, I still have a healthy fear of a substantial list of normal things. Like—I'm not taking up sky diving anytime soon. That would be more like a ninetieth birthday sort of feat when everyone (including me) is long past caring whether my landing is soft.

My point is the things I used to get worked up about just don't bother me anymore. I'm living the adage that life can change in a moment. So, I prepared for the meeting; it's not as though I winged it. I still have to do a good job. But I didn't have the presentation nerves I would normally have. And I ended up doing a great job. As I left the conference room, I experienced a warm sensation in my chest. A moment of pride mixed with pleasure. I hadn't felt anything like that in so long. It was odd. And unsettling. In that brief moment, I recognized a flicker of the old me. She was still in there—somewhere. Waiting.

Is Old Me ready to resurface? I still don't know. I was just so surprised and pleased to sense she's still in there somewhere, fighting her way through the dark forest. For nearly a year, I've felt abandoned in there. Lying in the dark in the fetal position. The ground is cold and damp. Though darkness surrounds me, I have never been able to lose consciousness. All this time, I have been fully alert for every moment of my terror. I have been excruciatingly aware of every drop of sorrow smothering me. Unable to break free yet knowing there was literally no one who could rescue me. No one can lead me out to the light. I have to find my own way.

Even with the wonderful friends I've had by my side this year, there is a point each day when I'm all alone. It's hard to learn how to live with that knowledge. Harder to imagine that someday, maybe we will be able to embrace the aloneness. Death doesn't allow us a choice in the matter. All we can do is choose how we will play the hand we've been dealt.

Even as I write this, I cringe at my word choice. Because death of a spouse is not something you can choose to bear. It's not something you can study for. It's not a test you can 'do well on'. It's a mind blowing, gut wrenching, heart shattering event you can't ever prepare for. It's a head on car wreck that could leave you paralyzed, or you may walk away from it. But, in no way are you unharmed. The internal damage can still slowly kill us.

There's no way to confidently assume we will find our way out of the forest. We can hope we will. We can pray we will. We may have others trying to drag us out. But until we know for ourselves- until

I discovered whether I would be strong enough to rise to my knees and start crawling toward the light, I couldn't know my fate. No one can truly know until they have to face it.

Maybe Old Me is ready to emerge? I don't know yet. I'm just seriously grateful to discover she's still in there. She's still fighting for me. For my beautiful girls— who need reassurance they didn't also lose their mom the night they lost their dad. For the first time, I think I can say with the tiniest measuring spoon of confidence—I'm going to make it. Just being able to say that feels like a damned lottery win.

Iris update: I held out my hand this morning before she approached, so she wouldn't startle. Today was the day. I touched her head! And Iris let me! Then she bolted. But it had me smiling when I left her room. I'm so excited for her. And proud of her courage. Sweet, little Iris wants more of a life than the quiet safety she has found under the bed, behind her closed door. Who knows? Maybe I want more than that, too?

###

11.5 months: **Small Improvements** With the anniversary of Dan's death looming, it's hard not to think of it with dread. The day my life was irrevocably changed in a horrific way. Before you ever lose someone, you only think of the remote possibility in shades of gray (when your brain allows you to go there). Your mind tries to cushion the blow— even of an imagined death. It's hazy and sad. You hope it won't be as terrifying as it feels when you're lying awake at night imagining his death. As you listen to your spouse snoring next to you.

What your brain fails to provide you with is the impact death has on the surviving spouse. My brain could never weigh the permanence of it. You imagine the 'what if'— but you don't play out the long term. You thump your snoring spouse, you think 'thank god' and you roll over and go back to sleep.

In the what-if scenario, you never have to play it out. To the awful discovery that it's worse than you ever could have imagined. It is so much scarier. So much harder. Yet, you somehow are managing to survive it. Widow's brain carries you through most of the first year— or at least the first six months. That foggy combination of excruciating grief and disbelief cushions the reality. But as we approach the one year mark, we start to examine the permanence of our new situation. The disbelief and grief are still there, but now they must be tempered by the *what-the-hell-am-I-going-to-do-now* mentality. Because the rest of your life is looming. Life is sitting there. Waiting for you to pick it up and move it down the field. While we can remain in a floundering state indefinitely, it's probably not good for us. Like a flu shot, it's best to take our medicine, ignore the sting and head back to work, even if we likely still resemble the walking dead.

I hung a little flag outside this morning. It's bright. It is cheerful. It has a picture of a buzzing bee with the message "bee happy". As I stood in Lowes contemplating it, I realized for the first time, I believe that's what I want to be. I want to be happy again. Last weekend I wandered the house, just noticing things. Maybe it's because for the past year I haven't noticed much of anything. For the last year, I have existed because I had to. I have eaten and slept because I had to do so to survive. But two nights ago, I noticed the drab, dark, worn out carpet runner in my foyer.

Last night I noticed the welcome mat was less than welcoming. Both of these items, I've likely had for a decade. Both are durable and functional and— completely dreary. So, today at lunch, I drove to Target and looked at welcome mats. I purchased a new carpet runner for my foyer. I bought two cheery yellow throw pillows for my sunroom. Tonight, I'll test them out to see if I like them.

I don't know if this is the start of a new trend. The *I-survived-the-worst-tragedy-of-my-life-and-I'm-still-standing* trend? Or whether I'm just tired after a year of sadness? Maybe I'll return everything tomorrow. (Note: I didn't). But for now, it feels a little like I've rounded a curve on the longest road I've ever traveled. I still think the anniversary is going to suck. I think it's going to set off a new round of anxiety. A new round of sadness and loss. A new wake-up call to the permanence of it all.

But then, I assume I'm going to pick myself up and take another step down the field. (Dan would love all these football analogies). I'm going to move the ball forward, inch by inch. Because that's what I have left. That's what we all have left. We all have to keep trying for that first down (okay, seriously—I'll stop). We don't get to just walk off the field— until it's our time to quit (Sorry. That's absolutely the last one). So, if I'm stuck here playing this crappy game; I think I want to start playing to win.

I think year two will also be a very difficult year, for completely different reasons. There is no magic pain relief at the achievement of 365 days without the person you couldn't bear to lose. Grief is still fresher than I'd imagined (or hoped) it would be. I suspect my loss will still equal pain in year two. But when doubt takes hold as to whether I can do it, I only have to look back to year one for a reminder on the strength and courage and endurance it took to slog this far. When I remember where I've been, I know I can keep going forward.

Iris update: Iris has decided over the past three days that I am friend rather than foe. She *greets me at the door* of her room now. She rubs against my legs, and she suddenly seems more interested in me than in the food I carry. Nearly four months in and I can finally pet her—from a sitting position on the floor. No sudden movements. No sounds. Coughing or sneezing will send her bolting under the bed. One night this week my stomach growled . . . and Iris glanced at me with accusation in her eyes.

Another rule: I am only allowed to pet her using one hand. I made the mistake of trying both hands on Sunday night and she was lost to me. Our moment was over as she sought refuge under the bed. Her golden eyes stared through me as though I'd broken our unspoken pact.

If I stick to one hand and I move very deliberately, I can get in a few pets and even a scratch or two while I talk very quietly. She will push her head into my hand and she even purrs. I sense a very sweet, loving soul under all the ratty hair and startled moves. I've started leaving her door cracked open to the hallway with a baby gate up so Ginger doesn't go all alpha cat on Iris' fragile sensibilities. But Ginger is fully aware of her now. She sits at the gate and stares at me the whole time I'm in Iris' room. At some point, they'll start sniffing each other; sizing each other up a bit.

I've started leaving the radio on for Iris so she can get used to hearing noise on a consistent basis. Even when I'm home, my house is too quiet. During the day when I'm gone, it's got to be so silent. When I think about the house she came from—eleven cats and an elderly woman who passed away . . . it's not surprising that noise makes her jumpy. But at some point, I want her to be comfortable integrating into the rest of the house. I want her to *want* to come out and explore. Sit with Ginger and me on the couch as we watch Hallmark movies on a Saturday night. Someday. I finally believe it's now possible for her.

# # #

Almost 12 months: Befriending Grief I've never felt the passage of time as acutely as I have this past year, lived in the early days one moment to the next. Minutes, hours, days. Then it became weeks. Now, I'm marking time in months. I guess this is progress of a sort.

One of the things I think I'm learning is that sometimes the hardest thing you can do is to just remain still. To not run away from grief. To not just lose yourself in all the things that keep you busy so you don't spend a night crying. But, running away doesn't work when you're carrying the grief inside. All you do is take it with you to the places you're trying to hide.

I noticed that this year, each time we ran away. When I'd run to DC to be with Chelsea. Or to Pittsburgh to be with Miranda. When we ran away for Thanksgiving and Dan's birthday and Christmas. It's not to say we were wrong to do that. I would maintain that we did what we had to, to get through the awful times. I would do it again. Running doesn't make you forget. You may achieve moments of reprieve. Moments of the normalness we crave when our lives have blown to hell.

This year has been the hardest of my life (so far). So many times, it would have been easier to give up; to wallow. To lash out. To embrace bitterness. To hate anyone who has "the perfect life" or hasn't experienced loss. So many times, it would have been easy to justify making impulsive decisions. I can't tell you how many times I stood in a store contemplating buying something. But each time, I asked myself whether that purchase would make me happier. Most of the time, that answer was 'no'. Nothing I could buy was going to make up for missing Dan. Nothing new would take away the ache in my heart. So, for better or worse, I haven't been much of a shopper this past year. Until lately, when I have bought a few items to lighten up my house—perhaps as my mood has gradually lifted.

Having survived this last year, I feel there is a danger to being impulsive—unless it's about people. I have gone with the impulse to finally fly home after four years of not having the time to get there. To visit my brother and my aging mother and extended family I've known all my life. I have given in to the impulse to financially help our girls—perhaps more than we did before. Because our lives are short.

This year I discovered it would have been easier to run away from what I was feeling. To chalk up my decisions to 'well, nothing matters anymore, so why not . . . (insert rash decision here). Buy a sports car. Sell my house. Quit my job and go live near my girls. Eat an entire cake in one sitting. Cash in my 401k and travel around the world. It's not that I don't still want to do those things one day—especially the travel. And definitely the cake! But sometimes, the hardest thing to do is absolutely nothing. To experience the impulse. The fear behind it. The need for—Security? Knowledge that I would one day be okay again? Closeness to my girls. Insert your own need here. Whatever it is, the hardest thing to do is ride it out. Resist it. Not the desire, but the impulse to have it right now. This moment.

Sometimes, you need to wander your lonely house until the sorrow finds you—surprising you as you round a corner. Sometimes, you need to just give in. To not fight against the wall of pain. Allow it to hit you; batter you; knock you to your knees. When it finally, finally recedes, like a wave rolling back out to sea; you'll have time to scramble back up. You'll have a few seconds to plant your feet. Just in time to greet the next incoming wave.

Throughout this first year I've been almost entirely alone to deal with my grief. My daughters live far away. They, too, have dealt with their pain mostly on their own. They have loving partners who have lessened it. Made it bearable. I am forever grateful to the loving, kind men my daughters have found. These men have eased their burden just a little.

This past year I haven't had anyone to share my pain. In an odd way, I'm sort of grateful for that now. Some days I was desperate to not be alone, yet by being alone, I've had endless time to process the raw, terrifying feelings. I've been able to release them; sort of like vomiting when you're sick. You dread the act; you know it's all coming up; you fight it for as long as you can, but boy do you feel better after you purge it. I've been able to beat back the cascading overwhelm that threatened to drown me. The terror there was absolutely no way I could do this great big, horrible thing on my own. This year, I've proved to myself I *can* do it. And that is some powerful feat, my friends. Take that grief, you big, scary bitch.

If the girls had been here with me, I think the year would have been less tough on me. Less tough on them. Yet would we have progressed very far in our grief? We absolutely would have provided each other strength and comfort. But would we also have just found ways to avoid dealing with our pain? I'll never know for sure. We would have been there for each other. We would have cried together, but likely not as much as I've cried on my own. We would have lifted each other up. But would we have learned to maybe avoid the grief? Running from the pain? Shopping and having fun just to get out of the house? I'm absolutely not criticizing the latter. We all must manage grief in our own way. For me, I think I needed to experience it; purge it; reflect on it and try to get back on my feet. I think I needed to purge all alone.

# # #

Hindsight 1: This first year is all about "just a little". If we can ask for "just a little" help. Have just a few good, true friends standing by us. We don't need legions. We need just a few loving family or friends who don't forget about us this first year. Whose thoughts turn to us—wondering if we need them. (We do). Wondering whether they can do something. Follow up on those thoughts. Because there is always something you can do. I'm not talking about re-roofing the house or taking out the trash or buying my groceries.

You can invite us out for coffee. Meet us at the gym. Invite us over to watch the big game. Take a walk through the neighborhood with us. See a movie with us. Share your Saturday morning at the farmers' market. It may be our only contact that day—or in many cases—for the entire weekend. I'm sure some of you are saying 'why don't you just tell us what you need'. That would be easier on everyone, wouldn't it? The truth is, we are too overwhelmed most days to ask for anything. We're depressed. We're foggy. We're exhausted. We know we need to see and talk to other people, but we can't summon the energy to ask. We can barely take care of ourselves. For the first several months, we're scraping by on autopilot. A 'normal' day of work, chores, kids, groceries— simple tasks are almost too much to bear.

I will be eternally grateful for the friends who have stuck by me. When you're drowning in grief, you long for something normal to break up the sadness. The 'normal' that other people take for granted. About two weeks after Dan died, one brave friend invited me to a lacrosse game on a Saturday afternoon. My stomach was in knots. I was so terrified to go. To be seen in public when it felt as though the rawness of my grief was spattered over me like red paint. What if I had a meltdown in public? When you have spent twenty-three hours a day crying, you're no longer certain you can hold it together. What if I ran into someone who knew Dan—but hadn't heard? A simple "How's Dan doing?" would have sent me over the edge. But that day ended up being a small miracle. Bright sun. A game to focus on. A few smiles. A comforting friend by my side who suspected how tough it might be. I got through it. I even enjoyed it. Most important—I was so proud of myself. For not bailing. A first *normal* event after my husband died. Two hours without crying.

In the early days especially, you need these small victories to begin restoring your confidence in yourself. That you can do this. Whatever *this* is. As an introvert, this was a hard task in life when I wasn't smothered in grief. That year I promised myself I would say 'yes' to just about any offer. Seriously unlike me. I'm a homebody. But I felt that if someone was kind enough to extend an invitation, then I could be brave enough to accept. The more I said yes, the more 'wins' I experienced in making it through an event without losing it. And the stronger I began to feel. Trust me, that first year, we need the confidence boost that we will survive this. I will survive it. You will, too.

Hindsight 2: Anniversaries will always be difficult. Each one will be painful and each one will likely be very different. As we age and change and gain distance from the trauma. But these days will always be fraught for me. There will always be an underlying tension as the anniversary approaches. Of what that day means. Of what happened. I will never be able to forget the day he died. His birthday. Our anniversary. I hope as the years pass, these days will become easier to remember. I hope they will mellow with time and I will get to remember all the good times versus the one very final bad time. How you handle them is the right way for you. I admire all the people I read about who plan such wonderful celebrations of their loved one's life. The creative ways they choose to honor their person. For me, thinking about ways to celebrate Dan just gives me anxiety. Even now, I just want to slink away and be alone on those days. I don't know how or if I will ever be able to recognize those hard days in celebration of Dan. But I so admire the people who are able to. Don't feel bad if you can't see your way around this. Maybe someday we will feel differently.

# # #

365 days: It's official. One year. 8,760 hours. 525,600 seconds. Those numbers don't really add up to me. It feels like a million hours. It feels like three years. And sometimes, it still feels like it happened yesterday.

Today has been harder than I imagined. I'd hoped I would experience a little relief . . . the kind you feel after a final exam. Thank God THAT's over. The feeling I had in college of *I'm-ready-to-move-on-to-a-new-class*. But instead, the day has been weighted with different emotions. Fresh grief— as though I've just said goodbye to Dan all over again. Guilt—because he's gone and I'm still here. Failure—having to live with the knowledge that I failed to recognize how bad the situation was that night. I've moved past the what-if-I-could-have-saved-him mentality, but I'm not sure I'll ever be able to hurdle the fact that he was alone. That he was likely terrified. That he got up from his seat and left us—because he knew it was bad. Yet, I—the person who knew him best in the world—failed to recognize it. Catastrophically failed to acknowledge the danger. It will be my lifelong regret that I wasn't there for him in his final moments. I should have been holding his hand. I should have been saying my last I love you's. Instead, he was all alone. And now, I will be too. I can only hope when my time comes, he'll be waiting for me on the other side and that he'll have forgiven me by then.

I know this next year will be different. Strange. Surreal still, yet possibly more real. More permanent. For better or worse, there's no longer a widow's fog clouding my brain or my actions anymore. But that means this year I will be facing the cold harsh reality of a life without Dan in it. Like it or not, this next year will be about me. About why I'm still here. About what I'm supposed to do with the block of time stretching before me. That will be weighty, fraught stuff to deal with. I won't have any excuses going forward; that it's too soon to be making decisions. I have no more hope left that his death was just a giant mistake and he'll be coming back.

Now, it's just me. And what I want to do. What I need to do for our girls. With our girls. I hate the idea of a new start. I hate the idea of new dreams—when I never, ever would have given up the ones we had. I adored our old life. I adored the stable, calm steadiness of it. I adored his laughter and spontaneity. His reliability and unwavering devotion. His trust in me and his trustworthiness. At eighteen and twenty, we grew up together. I loved the idea of us growing old together. Watching grandchildren grow up. I loved the plans we'd made. The dreams we shared.

We would have taken care of each other. Wholeheartedly. With unwavering devotion. In sickness and in health. We would have protected each other. Guarded each other's frailties. I loved our routine. Boring as an outsider may have viewed it. It was ours. And we cherished it. Even now, I weep at the vastness of my loss. If God could have taken anything else from us except our girls, I would give literally everything I own to go back to where we were before that night.

But that's not an option. Since this is the only life I have remaining, I will have to make the best of it— and I mean that in a good way. I want to live the best life I can. It's what Dan would have wanted and what I want, too. As battered and weary as I am, I want to be happy. Truly, I need to be. Because the last awful year isn't something I want to relive. I just want the days going forward to be less sad. To have the memories of him begin to comfort me and make me smile instead of cry. After a year of abject sadness, I am more than willing to try a new way to live.

The times I pray, it's for his happiness; that he's in heaven looking down at us; that he's somehow watching over us. That his early death was somehow worth it. That all this pain we've experienced this year was for a higher purpose. Dan always used to offer up his suffering for his mother. That it might help her get into heaven faster. I can only say that our collective pain should have launched him into heaven on a rocket—with a few side trips to the moon. If he is able to pray for us down here, I hope he is. This new life will probably be a bumpy ride. But I'll be hoping Dan is looking over our shoulders as we take each step.

Now, as I face year two, I feel stronger than before. I've gained a level of confidence that wasn't there six or seven months ago. I have found a level of peace that wasn't there even three months ago. Now, I rejoice at the knowledge that my faraway daughter is moving home. I look forward to having her close. But I'd like to think my reasons now come from a place of strength. That we don't want to waste another minute of our lives being far apart. That we want to celebrate our closeness by living near each other as we move forward.

At the worst time of my life, my little family was spread far apart, all living in different places. The times we could spend together were the best days of that first awful year. So often, we would wish we could be together. That if were in the same place—the same town—the same state, even—this year would have been easier. Not easier, exactly. But, less difficult. Because each time we were together, we felt a brief few days of 'normal'. A respite from our loss. As in, this awful thing has happened, but we are still holding up. We're smiling. We're laughing. We're hugging.

Those weekends were superpower weekends. We were united. And our strength together was so much more powerful than our individual strengths when we were far apart. But, as soon as my girls would leave me; or I would leave them, I would feel bereft, as though I'd suffered a new loss. As though I'd suddenly lost my right arm again. If we'd all been physically nearer to each other, would this pain have been easier?

As awful as the past year has been, I've been evaluating how it felt to do it all alone. Ultimately, I believe it was better that I had to endure the awfulness of Dan's death on my own. I've had a year to come to terms with it. I've had a year of not holding back. Of experiencing every awful feeling. Of giving in to a depth of sadness I never knew existed. At the end of the day, even your children can't take away your pain. No one can make it better for you.

# # #

Hindsight: That first year was so traumatizing. I'd never been in such a weakened state for so long. If my girls had been around, I likely would have burdened them with far more sadness than they could bear. While grieving themselves, I know they have worried endlessly about me, as I have about them. Had we all been physically close by, I believe in my heart that I might have leaned on them a little too much. I would have looked to them for distraction; for sympathy; for things they couldn't possibly give me— yet they would have tried their hardest to provide. I also might have attempted to quell my grief process—again, so they wouldn't worry. I would have cried in secret, swallowing it down until I was alone to deal with it. I think that would have slowed my process. Or maybe, I would've gotten stuck. Likely, I would've been happy to not think about it. To push it down. To take the easier path and bury the awful sadness. Who would voluntarily choose sadness if a distraction is readily available?

A year later, I actually feel grateful we have had to work through our grief on our own. Although that sounds counterintuitive, I hope it means we can now come together as equals. As warriors to this process. When one of us falters, we are collectively stronger and better able to help each other. If I'd had my girls to lean on, I don't think I'd be in the same place I am now. I hope I'm right in saying that. But what do I know? At the end of the day, I'm just bumbling along like everyone else.

# # #

12 months and one day: I've made it a year. I survived. I'm different from the person I was 366 days ago. Yet, Old Me is still here. I've seen more glimpses of her the last month than any time in the past year. She's still in the forest, but she's getting closer to emerging. She can see the light. She knows the way out. She's just taking her time on the journey.

A year later, I've realized I can continue asking why, but I'll continue to be disappointed. I can continue feeling bitter at the unbearable unfairness of it all. Some days I still do that. I am a work in progress. But I have opened the window to thinking about what's next. It's a beautiful spring morning. The breeze touches my face when I lean into it.

Instead of why—it's time to start asking what's next. I can spend my time bitter about the "friends" who never showed up or who dropped off the planet shortly after Dan's death or I can rejoice in all the amazing people who stood by our sides; who have loved and supported me; who have never allowed me to falter. The ones who carried me when I couldn't walk. The people who cared about me making it when I didn't care myself. I think every person reading this could tell the same story. We all have people we are thanking God for and others who we're thinking WTF—what the hell happened with them?

I was thinking recently about how Dan would have handled my death if this situation had been reversed. I would like to think he would have made it to this point still standing; that he would have summoned his unwavering belief in God; his adoration of our girls and his love for me. That he would have endured the unendurable. He would have called on his faith in God and he would be emerging from this awful tunnel with his gaze on the future. A corner of his heart still forever mine, but the rest of it open to possibility. To joy. To love. To kindness. To supporting our girls. Watching them forging through adulthood and cheering them on. He was the most generous, kind-hearted soul I've ever known. I know in my heart, he would still be that way, even in his sadness. I'm still unsure about my own belief in God. I know I still pray to him. I pray that Dan is with him because that's where he wanted to be. Dan's faith in God never wavered and mine has never wavered from Dan. So, maybe I'm halfway there.

# # #

What have I learned so far? I am stronger than I ever suspected—and strength comes in many forms. Some days, strength was just getting up in the morning. It was getting through a day at work without breaking down. Strength was breaking down at work and just going to the bathroom to regroup. I think everyone got used to seeing me with makeup on in the morning and red eyes by noon.

Strength was getting through a long, dark night. It was sleeping two or three hours and working myself to exhaustion, with the hope the next night would be better. Strength was facing a weekend with no plans. It was tackling the fear, hour by hour. What will I do to fill these hours? It was going to movies by myself and not caring what was playing. It was eating popcorn and pretending for a few hours that I was normal. I saw one movie three times. I'd seen it myself one Saturday when I was filling my hours. Then, a friend invited me to go. So, I went and saw it again. And then another friend wanted to see it, so I saw it a third time. When you are desperate for human contact; to be with friends for a few hours, you'll do just about anything. I wanted to be with people more than I cared about seeing a movie three times.

At the one-year point, I'm starting to be comfortable with being alone. I don't dread the weekends as much. I don't work as late as I did in the early days . . . afraid to go home. I have found that a routine helps. Going to the gym. Planning errands. Joining groups. Planning events with the women from my widows' group. Dinner or movies or concerts with friends.

Early on, my daughter reminded me it only takes a few scheduled events to get you through the weekend. A walk with a friend. A movie. Dinner out. As though she could sense the panic in my voice, Miranda reminded me she'd felt the same way when she moved to Pittsburgh knowing no one. It had taken her a while to hit a stride.

To find things to do to fill her weekends. To make friends. I hope that ultimately, I will become content with being alone, despite it not being my choice. I hope I will be able to find my new stride.

I have never enjoyed wallowing and this year has been a true test of that. The defeat that makes you want to give up; to rail against the unfairness that in the end—accomplishes nothing. I don't want to feel that way anymore. I want to be happy, though I have accepted it will be a different kind of happy. Not overjoyed. Not ecstatic. But, hopefully peaceful. Appreciative of what I still have, instead of grieving for everything I lost that night last March.

Another discovery I made, that despite the times we are living in, I realized people wanted to help us. So many people along this journey were there for me. Offering their assistance.

A few sucky things I've learned: All year long, I'd hoped for a Ghost-like revelation. As I type this, I feel a little nutty putting it down on paper. I really thought I'd get the chance to say goodbye; that Dan would somehow make his presence known to me. Before someone dies, if you think of death at all, you think about how there might be signs. Signals. The Patrick Swayze penny slide in Ghost. Or the glowing light that would confirm to me Dan was in a far better place; that all of my pain; our daughters' unbearable grief— that our unbelievable suffering had somehow been worth it because he was exquisitely happy. I'm still waiting on that sign. I guess that's what faith is supposed to provide us. For me, it is one more frustration.

Another disappointment: after a year of ugly crying, I can verify I've not gotten any better at it. Another Ghost aspirational reference—the perfect, Demi Moore cry. The beautiful, single tear trailing down a sculpted cheekbone with no red eyes. Yeah, that's never happened with me. It's a red-eyed, shoulder shaking, nose-running, ugly sob from the depths of your being. And there's nothing pretty about it.

It's half a box of tissues each time. I'm definitely more the 'can't cry pretty' of the Carrie Underwood song, than the perfection of Demi Moore in Ghost.

# # #

Hindsight 1: Accept the help that is offered. We only have to say 'yes'. We only have to ask— and let our friends assist us. But they are not mind readers. People want to help you, but they have absolutely no idea what we need. And they are afraid of us. Afraid of what we feel. Afraid of inadvertently tripping the wire to our grief. Wary of inadvertently hurting us more. So, we need to help them help us. Give them specifics—and let them help you. It will get easier for you to ask, I promise. And it will get easier for them to offer. We only have to ask.

Another biggie for me—I've discovered it's okay to need help. I just had to reach out. I had to seek it. Outside my comfort zone, for sure. I'm one of those people who likes to give help, but I never wanted to be on the receiving end. I had to make myself ask for it. And you know what happened? Countless people have helped me this year.

Ask your people. Lean on your friends. Lean on your family. Your neighbors. They will help you, I promise. This past year was not the time for gritty self-reliance. It wasn't the time to be tough. To be an island. Isolation is not good for us. This is the time we need to sit shiva. To coffee-klatch. To be around happy, normal people who are just living their happy, normal lives. Let them offer you a space at their table, if only for a night. This is a time to embrace anything that seems 'normal'. You will crave normal. Seek it out any way you can. Friends. Neighbors. Co-workers. I needed them all. You need them, too.

For all the people who wish to help the bereaved, my own experience has shown that kindness is never wrong and it's truly appreciated. I've learned that sometimes we can talk about our loved one and appear perfectly fine. And sometimes it hits us the wrong way. And I'm still surprised by it. One moment I think I'm fine. I can tell stories about Dan and laugh. The next minute, I can be sobbing. It will hit you out of the blue. I think it's safe to say that we'd rather risk you asking about our loved one. Because we obviously haven't forgotten the person we've lost. And if we cry on you, just give us a hug. We probably need it. Err on the side of kindness.

As I write this hindsight, we are still in the throes of the global COVID pandemic. 500,000 U.S. lives lost and counting. Millions of families and friends grieving the loss of someone close. Instead of the ripple effect of a stone tossed into a pond, we have become a nation of tsunami survivors. Of so many boulders being tossed into the pond that the giant waves of grief are flooding all of us. No one is safe from the crashing waves.

Before Dan passed, I was no different when it came to grief. We don't pay much attention until it happens to us. Tragic headlines serve more as an excuse to bury our heads into our own busy lives. Or to send up a quick prayer that it wasn't us. Until the lightning strikes you. It blasts your home. Your family. Your friends. A relative. And then it suddenly becomes painfully real. For all those who have lost someone to COVID, I am so sorry. Not only are you grieving, but you are also doing so largely alone. COVID has taken from us not only our loved one, but also the ability to say goodbye. To mourn with our families and friends. We are unable to gain closure nor to honor or family member the way we would like to. We are a nation of isolated mourners.

Hindsight 2: Grief counseling was incredibly helpful to me after the worst loss of my life. Meeting with a counselor can give you the opportunity to work though issues that you maybe can't share (or don't want to share) with others. For me, individual grief counseling was a starting point. Later, the widows' group counseling sessions and our monthly meetups were truly life altering. I will never be able to thank them enough for their support. If you're still reading this—please, please seek out counseling. It will help you. Our widows' group, forged from universal anguish has become a touchstone of strength for me, and hopefully for them. We are sisters in our loss.

Nearly three years after we started meeting, our widows' group meets to this day. In the middle of our grief process, the pandemic hit last year. The widows had to shut down for nearly nine months, but we kept in touch by email. When we got to the point where we missed seeing each other so much, we had to do something about it. Despite the odds, we are now meeting outside. Winter. Summer. We sit in a socially distanced circle; and we catch up on what's happening in our lives. The good, the bad, tough issues we face along with the celebrations. We lift each other up, we offer support and we lean on each other as we continue to hit our individual milestones. On the days when my strength can help someone, I am there for the others. And on the days when I don't want to get out of bed, I can count on someone else having a little strength to spare.

# # #

My one-year letter to Dan:

Well, I've made it. The girls have made it. We are battered, but still standing. Through the first year of the rest of my life without you. I hope you've been watching, as I pray you are. I don't want you to miss a moment of our beautiful girls' lives. There will be weddings and first houses and babies. I hate that you won't be here for any of it especially when it was all you ever talked about. About how much you wanted to be around for it. How your own father missed so much when he died young. And now, you're gone, too. So, I'm praying you can still see it all. That you can gaze down at your beautiful girls and continue being proud of them. There is so much of you in them. I see it every day.

It's not possible for a man with your heart to stop caring. When your heart stopped beating that night, mine shattered to bits. A year later, I sometimes feel as though it's still broken beyond repair. Other days, it feels as though the cracks are straining as they're held together with glue. Still other days—a little more often lately, my heart feels battered but still full of hope. Of fondness for the life we shared. Wistfulness, because I know I'll never share that again with anyone. My heart is full of gratefulness that I had 36 years with you. Yet, I still feel cheated we didn't get to celebrate the next twenty.

A year later, I feel honored to have known you (and surprised to discover I didn't know everything). I have come to believe and pray that you can't possibly have stopped knowing about us. You've sent us too many clues for us to ignore. Your songs to Chelsea on her way to work to let her know 'hey, I'm here with you. Drive safe to work'. The songs you send me when I'm at a low point. Your timing is impeccable. We always called you Captain Obvious and you're still living up to that moniker. At the beginning, I said I couldn't feel your presence. I was angry about that, I wanted Ghost. I wanted to see you. To feel you. To talk with you one last time. To hold your hand and say all the loving words I would have said if I'd known they

WERE our last words. Instead, you had jokes. Teasing about why you couldn't sit still and watch the game you loved. If there was a warning to be had, I'm so unbelievably sorry to say I missed it.

If I'd only known... the last time I held your hand was at the hospital when it was too late. Your hand still warm but achingly still. Your voice silent when I begged you for answers. Your beautiful, blue eyes were closed when I wanted them smiling at me. Through the miracle of organ donation, I hope they are smiling at someone else now—not that I would ever want to hear from them to thank me. Because I still can't bear the thought of your eyes smiling at someone else.

I hope you will someday be able to send us signs. Believe me, we're searching hard for them down here. Snippets at the low points. Things that stop the sobs and create a brief smile. Clues that make me sense you're here with me. The sensation of rightness that quiets my doubt. When I question whether I'm doing the right thing— I imagine you cheering me on. Reassuring me that *I've got this.* I've got the girls, Babe. God willing, I won't drop the ball with them. We worked too hard and loved them too much for me to allow them to fall. We each may stumble from time to time, but we will not allow any of us to fall down.

This year without you has proven many things. I are weak and I am strong. I am scared. And I am fearless. We have questioned so much. Yet, we still have faith. In you. In ourselves. And yes—in some kind of higher power.

To fill my time and try to find some peace, I've tried painting. Believe me, you'd be laughing your ass off if you could see the results. And no—I don't anticipate improving with time. After knowing you for 36 years, I think I can anticipate your comments. "Maybe you should stick to writing" or "they don't look THAT bad" or "if you let me hang a Tom Brady poster, I'll agree to let you hang *that* up."

I still haven't been able to attend another game at the ballpark where you left me. Though we spent happy times there, I still associate the place with the event. I still flash back to you walking away from me. That quiver of fear I experienced— as though I could sense something terrible was about to go down. So, while I can't see a game there, I'm happy to report that the girls have been to games in other places. Maybe I will, too, eventually. Last summer, my grief counselor pointed out that attending a ballgame is not actually necessary to my existence. It's not as though I fear eating vegetables. It's a damned ballpark—one that should have had defibrillators available to possibly save you. Knowing what I do now about Virginia athletic events and the paltry lack of laws to force sports arenas to comply with even the most basic safety standards, I have trouble imagining attending any event at a sports park. But you don't want to hear me rant about things that can't be changed.

Your love of sports won't die, Dan because ultimately, I can't give up something that gave you so much pleasure, nor a place where I might get an opportunity to sense your presence. Don't laugh—but my grief counselor suggested I might want to take up coaching a team someday. Like you did. Or sponsoring one. Maybe the girls and I could coach a little girls' softball team—just as you did for all those years with our girls. I doubt I could live up to the Coach Creampuff reputation you had, but I can try to be as kind and thoughtful as you always were. I'll have to report back on that one. But it's a nice idea, isn't it?

I hope my decisions this past year would agree with you. After 36 years together we always listened first before chiming in with our opinions. I've tried to practice the WWDD method. What Would Dan Do? What would the kindest man I've ever known want me to do? Then, if I'm still stuck, I always know how to decide. I err on the side of kindness. On the side of spontaneity. Of go-for-it. Of your famous you-only-live-once generosity. Of saying yes instead of no. Of helping someone. Of giving someone the benefit of doubt. Of having faith in others. Of the Holy Spirit that lived inside you.

When I perform this exercise, the clouds shift and the light pierces through the darkness. And I know what to do. It's perhaps not the most practical way to make decisions, (of which I've always had an abundance). But it's always the right way. So, thank you for that. I'm signing off for now. I love you and always will. I hope you're watching, but if you're not, I'm taking good notes. As you often (thankfully) said to me . . . 'I'll see you on the other side'. I truly hope that's true. Those words have provided endless comfort over the past year. You'd better be waiting for me because we are going to have tons to catch up on. Love you always.

# # #

Twelve months and two weeks: Having plans isn't a bad thing, as long as we realize they may never come to fruition. That first year has been a swirl of emotions beyond grief. Fears. Wishes. Dreams. Plans. There's a reason why we are counseled to hold off on the heavy decisions. I think it's because too much is in flux. We are reactive. Operating from a place of terror. From a place of overwhelming sadness. Anxiety about the future. Personally, I'm still triggered by certain things and even my triggers seem to be changeable. And they come without warning. That suggests to me that I may not be in the best frame of mind to make critical decisions.

The experts say you shouldn't make major changes after a death. But isn't death the most enormous change one could ever be thrust into? In a single moment, Dan lost his life and I lost mine too. The one we planned. And worked for and saved for. The life where we sacrificed and scrimped in the short term to savor the fruits later. The later he never got to experience.

Frankly, since Dan left, I feel every decision has been major. Overwhelming. Possibly life-altering. Questioning myself every step of the way. One thing I have learned is if I can't postpone the decision, then I make the decision that feels the most right. Or—the least wrong. I've learned to ask myself 'will I regret it if I don't do this?"

It's certainly not a foolproof way to make decisions, but it helped me overcome my inertia when it came to a few difficult decisions. Like spending money on a long term care plan. Weighing the cost of it (wicked expensive) versus the burden I could potentially place on the girls if I didn't spend that money now. After surviving this year without Dan, I don't want the girls to suffer a decision on my behalf if I can do something to help them with it now.

For a planner like me, my new way of doing things sometimes makes me a little crazy. I long for something to feel substantial again. I would love to have a plan I felt confident about. Perhaps that would allow me to move forward? Would a solid plan make me happy? Or would it just be another form of running away? Pretending I'm back on track because "I have a plan"? Maybe the master plan is to NOT plan. For now. I don't think I can create a spreadsheet that makes the future look brighter. At least not yet. I can't research a new place when I'm not ready to leave the old one. When I don't know where I'm going. My house is a comforting burden right now. Laden with happy memories and now, with my quiet sadness. I can't leave it yet. I don't want to leave it yet. I guess—that is a decision, right? I'm staying put. For now.

At the one-year point, I still don't know what I want—except to make this constant ache in my chest go away. So, I'm waiting. I need to settle—whatever that means. But *settle* is the word that feels right. I need to calm. I need to be patient with myself and with my decisions. Rushing won't take the ache away and might just make things worse if I launch into a half-baked plan that *might* make me happy. Emphasis on the might. This past year has been about adapting. Adjusting. My expectations of myself and others.

Ultimately, I will find a new dream— which I'm no closer to figuring out. After nearly four decades of being a duo—I knew who I was as half of a couple. But, on my own? Not so much. I was eighteen when I met Dan. Now, I'm fifty-five. Who am I? I have no idea yet. Something is emerging from the cocoon after a year on my own. It may be a butterfly or a giant, mutant bug. I'm not even sure yet whether I'll like her or not. The past twelve months have been about tweaking. My hopes. My expectations. Even my beliefs. I'm not the same person I was twelve months ago.

# # #

Iris Update: Every morning as I pack up my yogurt and salad and get ready to head off to work, I hear Iris running back and forth over my head. Her two-room suite is apparently enough distance for her to work her way up to a full gallop. She runs back and forth for at least ten minutes. Hearing her overhead makes me smile. There is a personality trapped inside there. Increasingly, I find myself wanting to discover it.

I learned this week that Iris doesn't quite know how to play. I have a toy on a stick that I try to drag (very slowly) on the floor when I'm sitting there, petting her slowly. The first time I dragged the toy, it slithered like a snake across the carpet. But instead of pouncing, Iris bolted—this time up on top of the bed. Ginger loves this toy, but Iris is terrified of it. So that got me started on testing a series of toys. She likes balls, especially rubber ones that bounce. She will chase it into the spare room but then is uncertain what she's supposed to do with it.

At first, my goal was to get Iris socialized enough to be adoptable. But, I'm not sure that will ever be possible. She's still incredibly skittish; afraid of her own shadow. A wounded soul. Basically, a lot like me. But I see a hint of courage. Glimpses of a cute, friendly personality.

It is common in animal shelters that older cats, even those with great personalities, have trouble competing in the adoption race with hordes of adorable kittens. Older cats are a tougher sell. And then there's Iris. Poor, shlubby Iris is guesstimated to be around four years old. She can't be touched. She doesn't say much and her favorite activity is cowering under the bed. A sneeze will send her under there for ten minutes.

I would love to be able to groom her, but that's just a fantasy at this point. I've tried. I've gotten as far as lifting the brush to her head before she recoils and runs. Her long, tortie hair has the potential to be pretty. She's mostly black, but with lots of peachy orange on her belly. But we're four months in now and she still looks pretty scruffy. One day we're going to see the princess emerge from her rough and tumble tomboy roots. Or it may just be that I've been watching too many Hallmark movies to be this hopeful about my slow burn relationship with Iris.

I'm starting to worry a tiny bit about Miranda's big, fratty boy cats moving back home in the next month or so. If cats could play sports, Miranda's boys would be rugby players. Ginger would be a ballerina. And Iris would play whatever sport could take place in the four-inch space under the bed. Jig saw puzzler? Will my Iris face a setback with these ruffians? Will Ginger? My Ginger girl rules the house. Will her ego take a blow with the frat boys moving in?

I realize now that my attempt at fostering these girls was pure folly, because let's face it, there's no way I can give them back. Last night I was scrolling Facebook and saw Ginger's face in the humane society's ad—stating she was still available for adoption. My heart started pounding so fast. It was like seeing one of my kids' faces on a For Sale poster. How can I possibly give her up when she's become my best friend? I was crying as I started to type up the online adoption application so I wouldn't lose her overnight to another applicant. Before I could lock her down. I should have known how this would play out. Every Saturday, I would make excuses as to why I couldn't take Ginger to the adoption stand. And with Iris, I wouldn't have been able to catch her to put her in a carrier, even if I'd wanted her to go.

Ginger may be my soulmate, but increasingly, I sense Iris is my spirit animal. We've come a long way together. We're both still pretty damaged. After being broken into a million tiny pieces, we've been glued back together. But the sum of us is still weaker than the parts. Sensitive to any pressure. The glue hasn't dried. One good fumble and we'd probably collapse in on ourselves. However, we're both plucky. We've picked ourselves off the floor this year. Adapted to new situations. We are forging ahead despite our fear of the unknown. I'm suspecting I might need to keep Iris, too.

# # #

Hindsight: At the one-year point (or longer) it is okay to not have any answers. 'I don't know' IS an answer. It's still my go-to answer most of the time now, at the almost three-year point. But in that awful first year, 'I don't know' was pretty much the only answer. It's the perfect answer. But it's hard to sit back and wait. It's hard to just 'be'. For a planner and a problem-solver, it was very difficult for me to do nothing. It still is. But as I do nothing, I'm buying time to see how my life plays out. Where will my kids land? When will I want to leave my job and move on to something else? At the end of the day, my decisions need to be about me and what I want. Until I know what that is, I'm best to stay put and keep treading water.

# # #

13 months: Moving Forward My daughter has moved back in with me. I am overjoyed to have her back. More than her being home with me, she's home from Pittsburgh. She is no longer six hours away from me and Chelsea. While she is under my roof again, no matter how temporary, I am going to enjoy every moment of it. Along with her, she has brought the Frat Boys. Her two boy cats who have, over the years, dominated the house. During grad school, Ran left them with us while she was gone for several months on an internship. When not sleeping, they would rampage through the house. The quiet, empty-nester house that Dan and I had grown used to. They'd leave hair and hairballs on the rug. They knocked over lamps while chasing each other up and down the stairs. For me, this was great fun. For Dan? Not so much. But like the wonderful dad he was, he made the best of it. Why? Because taking on the Frat Boys was helping our daughter.

Now, the boys are back. Integrating them with the two girls is out of the question. For one thing, Iris is still upstairs, confined to one room. For her, the boys' arrival doesn't change much. For Ginger, it's a different story. To say she is deeply offended by the Frat Boys' presence is probably understating it. Ginger is a tiny girl with a big hiss. She is no match for two boys who are twice her size. She is outnumbered and outweighed. But she has been straining to attack them for the weeks they have been back.

Since the living situation is temporary, we are keeping them separated. Will that make for a long, tedious dynamic each day? Yes. But my daughter and I both have to work and we both want to come home to the same number of healthy cats each night. So, we can't allow bloody catfight rumbles to occur during the day while we're gone. So, the Frat Boys and Ginger will have their share of lockdown time to allow the other to roam free. Like Ran and me, they will all make the best of it. Ginger has made her position on the matter abundantly clear. For the last two weeks she has very deliberately taken a dump outside the litter box a couple times a week. I respect her opinion. Big, smelly poops—just for me.

# # #

Hindsight: If I'd ever wondered how many cats are too many? My answer now would be four cats who don't know each other are definitely *way* too many cats. I don't know how Iris survived in a house with eleven cats. Maybe that's why she's so easygoing. She's seen much, much worse—and this situation is a veritable cakewalk.

# # #

15 months: **Renewed Friendship** I am taking a brief respite from my grief journey to take the trip of a lifetime with the girls. I'd always talked with Dan about taking the girls to Europe at least once. Before husbands and houses and babies (hopefully) arrive on the scene. For his part, Dan hated to fly. He would avoid it at any cost. So, it's not as though he would be missing this trip the girls and I are taking together. He would have been so excited for us. He would have been nervous about us flying, but so joyful about the adventure we would have. The girls and I have been planning since Thanksgiving. We discussed a trip; I suggested a few places and then let them decide. The unanimous decision was Italy. I've only been there once—and that was five years ago. Despite my love of travel and my yearning to see all of Europe eventually, the fact remains that I'd never been anywhere until my fifties. And that trip only happened when Dan's mother passed away and left him a share of her house. In typical Dan fashion, he insisted I use some of the money to take a trip to Italy. There had never been money to do something so frivolous just for myself. Between paying bills and saving for college, I couldn't have brought myself to splurge like that. So, Dan made it happen for me.

This time around, I am making it happen for our girls. I want us to enjoy the hell out of it. We've obviously learned how fleeting time is and we all want to make the most of it. A surprise addition to our group: Dan's sister. She lives across the country from us. Her visits during the girls' growing up years were scarce. Expense. Distance. Work and the pull of her own life made her a distant but loved aunt and sister-in-law. She took Dan's death very hard. They were very close, speaking by phone or texting pretty much every week. Though she was out of sight, she was never out of mind.

The in-law relationship is an interesting animal. Mary and I have been friends for decades. We worked together for a bit before she and her then boyfriend, now husband, left for the opposite coast thirty-odd years ago. Since then, my relationship with her had become funneled through Dan. He relayed messages back and forth between us. It wasn't a deliberate act, this not speaking for years at a time. It was just the Dan filter of him *always* speaking with her and me saying "oh, tell Mary this . . ." and "don't forget to mention that . . ." So, the phone call to tell her that her younger brother had died was obviously a blindside that no one ever saw coming. It has also made us both feel a little like strangers as we now come together with no Dan to keep us updated on each other.

She traveled east for his funeral and stayed with the girls and me for a few days. But those blurry, awful, early days weren't much of a visit. It was a zombie fest of us moving gingerly through space and time. Still, I appreciated her desire to spend time with us and the effort she made to stay with us. It had to have been so painful for her. Yet, she reconnected with the girls, which was lovely. They regained an aunt they hadn't seen much while growing up. She visited again several months after Dan died. It was good to see her and to catch up. Chelsea also traveled west to visit a friend and spent a few days with her aunt. I know Chelsea was happy to see her and I think Mary enjoyed it as well.

In that spirit, I asked the girls at Thanksgiving if they would like to invite their aunt to travel with us to Italy. I felt she might jump at the chance of a fun trip with the girls and the chance to see her own father's homeland in southern Italy. The girls were excited about asking her along. It turned out Mary was excited about going with us. So, the four of us have now embarked on our whirlwind tour of Italy. A tourist sampler so we can see as much as possible in eleven days. The girls and I will be in a triple room. Cue the soundtrack to Psycho . . .

Mary has very wisely chosen to upgrade to a single. We've only just boarded the plane to Rome, and I already envy her. The girls and I have set rules for ourselves. Due to the close quarters, we've agreed that no one can be allowed to get so moody that they ruin any aspect of this trip. Not that I have much estrogen left, but the girls have plenty enough to go around. I know I personally will be battling grief in uncomfortable moments when I can't hide from them. So, we'll all have our moods to deal with. I've also spent a small fortune on this trip for the three of us. Everyone has sworn to be on our best behavior. Say a prayer for us.

# # #

Hindsight: The trip to Italy was glorious. There were several moments of sadness for me, but I handled those moments as quietly as possible. Usually in the bathroom in the middle of the night. Traveling with Mary was a wonderful idea that I know added special memories for all of us. Sometimes it was hard, being around a person so very much like Dan. Her mannerisms are so, so similar. Her laugh. Her sense of humor. Even down to the way she holds her fork. Sometimes it felt good to see flashes of him in someone else. Like all moments of grief so far, sometimes it hits you harder than you expect and sometimes you're okay with it.

As I write this now, I am so grateful for our big trip. We traveled to Italy in July, 2019. Six months later, in January 2020, the world watched, horrified as Italy followed China in being ravaged by the pandemic. An explosion of cases; overrun hospitals and a shocking number of deaths in the breathtaking regions we'd only recently returned from. As I watched the horror unfolding each night on the news, my gut tightened with dread over what I knew we would shortly face ourselves when COVID started taking hold here in the US. I hold the memories of our trip near to my heart. I know I will return to Italy again. I pray it will be soon.

# # #

17 months: **Grim acceptance** I would say that keeping this diary was a form of therapy of sorts. But that would be implying that I now feel better after doing so. To me, the term 'therapy' suggests you can improve. You can overcome what is bothering you; you can learn to live with whatever ails you. In my case, that hasn't happened. 17

months in, all I can really say is that I've survived. I guess that's what we get to tell ourselves.

At twelve months, I used the rationale that I've made it thru the worst year of my life; that can only mean I'll be able to get thru year two, right? Because it couldn't possibly be any worse than Year 1 was. That is partially an accurate statement. Year 2 is different. There is less moment to moment anguish. There are fewer panic attacks. Fewer moments when I struggle to breathe. I still have plenty of anguish, tears, panic attacks and moments when I feel as though I'm suffocating, but the good news is that I find I am slightly better able to regain control when I unleash these symptoms of my grief.

The other big issue "normal" people forget (thru no fault of their own) is that survival mode and "moving forward" are very different. I haven't moved forward yet. Or if I have, I haven't moved very far. That remains a mysterious future accomplishment for me. I look forward to it. I pray for it. But at the 17-month point, I'm still in the WTF happened to me stage. A bomb went off seventeen months ago. After the smoke finally cleared, I discovered I've survived the initial explosion. However, I'm still desperately missing the parts of me that blew off in the explosion. I need them. I want them back.

Excruciating phantom pain suggests my parts still exist. My brain can now understand the body part is long gone. I am no longer clouded by the thick, bewildering fog of shock and grief. I am able to think clearly. I am able to see the long stretch of future that awaits me. And some days, that clarity is so much more unbearable than the numbness of last year.

# # #

18 months: The Medium I have hit a bizarre point in my healing process. To explain this, I have to go back a bit in time. One night six months ago, one of the widows mentioned that they'd been to see a medium. We were all very curious how the experience turned out. She'd had a positive experience and gained several messages from her husband and/or details of their lives that the medium could never have known. I was a little floored by the conversation about her experience. Before that moment, I'd never given any thought at all to the idea of a medium. Pragmatist here—remember? So, literally no thought EVER of the possibility of being able to summon his presence.

So, it turns out a medium is the person (like the big-haired woman on TV) who can summon the spirits of your loved ones to show up and she/he can then translate what they are telling you. I'd never seen the show Long Island Medium, but I'd seen commercials, so my expectation was of a shlocky sort of surface experience that would cost a great deal but yield next to nothing in insight. No disrespect intended. Just my gut feeling.

After hearing that night that one of our members had appreciated her experience made me try to think about it in a less skeptical way. If Dan hadn't died, I doubt I would have ever thought about researching mediums, let alone contemplated visiting one. But here we are. Another member of our group immediately booked an appointment with the same woman. It was a six month wait. I couldn't shake the idea that maybe I should try it, if only to snuff out the curiosity it had raised. So, I bought a book on mediums that one of the widows had read and recommended. (We did this a lot with books). If any of us read something we found helpful, we passed them along to the others to read. As I began reading the book, I went ahead and made an appointment with the medium the other widow had seen. Six months later, that appointment was this week.

In the meantime, I'd read the skeptic book on mediums (see resources) and one of the books written by the Long Island medium of TV fame (see resources). I'd wanted to learn as much as possible before my appointment so I could be prepared for what to expect. I couldn't shake the slightly desperate feeling that I might be going a little crazy. But it was blended with a compulsive need-to-know. Why was I—theoretically of sound mind—doing something like this? But I couldn't shake the impulse to do it, now that I'd heard about it. This had become something I had to explore, or I'd always wonder. And I now had two women whose opinions I value, say it was an experience they'd appreciated and gained comfort from. So, I was about to embark on the same adventure.

It turned out to be both as odd as I'd imagined and later, comforting. Going through it was exhausting because I basically cried through the whole thing. But I was able to go back later and evaluate what she'd told me, and like the others, there was too much there for me to be able to dismiss. For starters, the medium, after introductions and explanations, gave me a strange look and said "Dan is here and he's cracking up. He's saying in a million years, he'd never expect you to do this". Maybe that's something the medium opens with all the time to break down the skeptics. But for me, it sort of hit the nail on the head because it was exactly what I was thinking myself.

The hour passed very quickly. I was both drained and relieved when it was over. Yet as I replayed her conversation and the messages passed to me, I can say the session was also a source of comfort in the weeks after. I felt the slightest modicum of closure I never received the night he died. I don't know that I would go again. I'm not sure what more visits would yield for me. I can see where the sliver of peace you receive in that hour might make you want to return again. However, I'm not sure I would be willing to risk wandering down that rabbit hole. I know I need to move forward. Continuing to seek out the past is not going to get me there.

# # #

Hindsight: I am truly glad I tried something that was so wildly unlike me and out of my comfort zone. I do feel Dan was present during that session. The medium told me things she couldn't possibly know about us. And the messages 'sounded' like Dan. I was nervous to tell the girls about my visit, concerned they would assume I'd taken leave of my sanity. Though they were surprised I would think of something like that, they were quickly fascinated and wanted to hear everything I'd learned. If anything, they'd wished they could have gone with me. One of my daughters has since gone to a medium to see if she would learn anything that might bring a little comfort. Though she received several messages, her takeaway was that the information wasn't specific enough for her. She wanted a clear-cut sign instead of little snippets of information.

One thing I'd neglected to tell her was that in my readings on the subject, I'd learned that oftentimes a medium will give you messages for other people in your life. You, the receiver are obligated to pass those messages along. For instance, my medium had given me a message for my mother from my bastard father. I passed it along to her—that he was "sorry for being such a terrible husband". Her response? "Too little, too late".

My daughter received messages from her medium about me. She told my daughter it was my birthday that day. (It was). Another was that I was a writer—something the medium couldn't possibly have known. One of the messages from Dan was "tell Mom she needs to write her story". Though my daughter was not very impressed with this message, I admit to being startled by it. Since Dan died, I've been unable to write my stories. But I have been keeping this diary. So here I am—telling my story. Perhaps someday we'll all visit a medium together. When more time has passed, and the visit won't be so fraught with regret and sadness and the search for meaning.

As for recommendations, I still think visiting a medium may provide comfort to those who find themselves stuck in their grief or like me, those who have unanswered questions. I would recommend doing some research on the subject of mediums and check reviews if you decide to visit one. At least make sure you will get a decent experience for the money you pay. Who knows? Maybe it will provide a level of comfort. I've learned through this process that I need to keep an open mind about things.

# # #

19 months: My toddler aged grief is still with me. Like a growing child versus an infant, I know him much better now. I know his triggers. My entire goal some days is one of desperation to avoid anything that will set off a tantrum. To experience one day without exhausting incidents. To have a day when I don't break down for the thousandth time. Yet, some days I can still be completely blindsided by sorrow. Grief, you're such a bastard. On those tiring days, I just give in. To the whiny, sobbing tantrum, to the hopeless anguish I still feel when I let my guard down. Those days, I regress all the way back to the infant grief you used to be.

I gave birth to this grief, and I will grow old with it. But unlike a baby growing to adulthood, whose progress I can measure and marvel at, this emptiness is something I drag along behind me each day. A ball and chain I acknowledge I will never be entirely free of. My hope is that my legs will eventually strengthen enough that I won't feel the burden of your weight. That one day, the chain clanging against my leg as I drag you along will not be quite so noticeable.

Friday nights are still hard. Not that the other days aren't difficult, but there's something about a Friday night. The workday winds down. Everyone is eager with anticipation for a couple well-deserved days off. Me? I approach them with less of last year's terror, but with a still respectable level of dread. What used to bring such joy and relief at the end of a stressful work week still makes me panicky. Can I fill all those hours? Will I be alone all weekend? Will I enjoy the time away from work? At this stage, it's still questionable. Some weekends I actually have fun. I enjoy the time off; the hours go fast. I sleep well. Or some end up like this one. Friday night and I'm alone on the couch eating takeout soup and watching a Hallmark Christmas movie I've seen five times. It's not that I'm miserable, exactly. Just a raw-edged awareness that this is not the life I was supposed to be living.

Dan isn't here to make jokey comments. He can't whine that I've seen this movie a hundred times, right before he would plop down and watch it with me. We used to share a simple dinner on Friday nights. Neither of us wanting to cook; him coming home late from the gym. We'd usually split a sub. Have a drink together. Go to bed early or stay up late and sleep in on Saturday. I miss those little things. Though I miss every part of our lives, I miss tiny moments the most. The everyday, mundane conversations we shared. Listening to each other. He would always make me laugh with a funny observation or a quick joke. I loved our time together so much. I miss you so much, Dan. Ginger cat patiently listens to my snarky comments about the movie characters, but she doesn't *really* appreciate them. As I watch this stupid movie for the hundred and first time, I can't help aching once again over how much I've lost.

# # #

20 months: Life Moves Forward Our daughter got engaged today. I'd known for several months it was coming. Her fiancé was planning and plotting, waiting for the perfect moment. Today was that day. Oh Dan, she is so happy. And I'm so happy for them. They will have a wonderful life together. They are right for each other in all the important ways. To say they remind me of us would sound trite, but I actually do believe it. They are kind to each other. They make each other laugh and they are each other's fiercest backer and best friend. They have already faced both good and terrible together. They have plowed through adversity and setbacks and they are stronger than ever. He has comforted her through the awful times she has experienced since Dan's death. He is perfect for her. I pray Dan is aware of all this, because I'm not really doing the news justice tonight. The joy I experienced at their happiness, tempered by the fact that as I drove home, he wasn't there to celebrate this first milestone with me. The first of many to come that he will miss.

In some ways, my heart is breaking all over again, but I pray this sadness will not overtake the true joy I feel for them. This weekend Miranda, too, is moving back out on her own. A momentous weekend all around. I'd like to think I will handle being alone again better than the first time around. It has been so wonderful to have her here with me these last six months. I believe the time was made sweeter because I knew it would only be temporary.

She spent six months here with me as she organized her future. Despite my current weeping over her departure, I feel stronger today than before she arrived. I've changed so much, yet on the outside I feel I look the same. Inside, there's a permanent hole in my heart, a sadness I haven't been able to shake. Maybe it's there forever. I guess I'll only find out as I continue to travel this road. At the same time, I have experienced happiness. These moments always catch me by surprise, because it has been so long since I have truly laughed or smiled or felt real joy. Today was one of those days.

Tonight, my joy makes me sad if that makes any sense. Because it means I'm moving on. I survived a cataclysmic event; one that has forever changed me. Yet, I've learned I can still feel happy. I can still laugh. I can still hope, for our girls . . . and finally, for me. I will have some form of a good life. Whatever form it takes, it will be mine to stamp in a way I choose. I will finish the job we started together and get us over the finish line. As I continue to gain strength, I'm discovering the ability to find happiness in small moments.

Iris update: My sweet, terrified girl is DOWNSTAIRS with me right now. Curious, as she bravely explores the first floor of the house she has never seen since she arrived nearly a year ago. She was ready for this big step several months ago, had it not been for the arrival of the Frat Boys. Iris has patiently waited for this moment. As she inches away from the stairs, her courage is stronger than her fear of the unknown. She wanders from room to room, sniffing everything. A whole new world has opened up to her and she is so very curious. Every few minutes, she seems to sense how far she has strayed from the stairs and she scurries back to them. But then, a moment later, she is on her way again, exploring another room.

I am so proud of her. Ginger is still not thrilled with the idea of Iris having freedom to wander the entire house, so I'm keeping an eye on her. Letting Iris explore and discover without the worry of Ginger pouncing on her. As she leaves her scent downstairs, I'm hopeful Ginger will accept the message that Iris is here to stay. That she belongs in this odd little family we've formed.

Watching Iris wander makes me realize how far she's come from the traumatized, wounded girl who arrived last November. How far I've come as well. It reminds me that we're all in this together. The girls and I will all make it together. As my daughters embark on their new lives, I will continue to be there for them. As I slowly, feet-dragging, tentatively embark on my new life, I know they will be cheering me on, too. Always closely tethered, even if we're not all in the same place. We've survived physical distance for this long. We'll continue to make it as we move forward. Always together in spirit and love. I think Dan would be happy about that.

# # #

2 years: Another Milestone I've made it through another anniversary. This one painful, but thankfully muted when compared with the first-year marker. I'm relieved, actually. It's hard to maintain the level of anguish I've endured the past two years. I'm truly hopeful this means I'm on the path of resigned acceptance. Of sorrow that still visits often, but the stays are shorter. An unwanted guest who disrupts my life, but then quietly slips out the door rather than suffocating me with my pillow in the night. I got through much of this second year by reminding myself about the first. If I made it through the first year . . . it must mean I can make it through the second. Not exactly confidence-inspiring, but I've learned to make do with the tools I have. I now embark on year 3 spouting the same platitudes that have gotten me this far. Year three will likely be more bearable than year 2. Let's all hope, shall we?

This anniversary has been overshadowed by the global pandemic that has begun leaving its mark on the world and now, the United States. I wonder how this new, scary, isolating enemy will affect us all. I have the feeling it will have a more devastating impact on us than we are willing to imagine right now. I've often wondered whether our generation would experience something catastrophic like the Spanish Flu a century ago. Several years ago, I thought the bird flu would be the "big one". But it thankfully petered out without much global damage, and I got lulled into a false sense of complacency that maybe it couldn't happen to us. We're so "advanced" and globally dominant that our scientists and government would be all over it if such a terrible illness appeared. Now, I wonder if this will be the thing that takes us all out. A combination of political rhetoric, governmental paralysis and a heightened "me first" arrogance that we have become famous for the past few years.

It's hard to imagine having to give up the few baby steps forward I've been able to accomplish. The gym has become something of a lifeline for me. A solid part of my routine to keep me strong and busy for chunks of time. The widows' group I have come to rely on. We meet only once a month, but it is a very necessary social crutch for me. Seeing the women who continue to survive after loss. We lift each other up. We appreciate how far we've come from where we were at the start of our individual nightmares. The friends I now see a few times a month for dinner and a movie. Or dinner and a play. Or old, classic movies at the theatre. I have grown to appreciate the need to keep myself out there with events that remind me I'm still alive and I need to socialize. One thing the pandemic has brought to light? I've come a lot farther than I gave myself credit for. I pray this new isolation doesn't erode the altered life I've begun to forge for myself.

For so long, I didn't really care whether I was still around. I still feel that way, for the most part. I've been isolated for the last two years. Not much of that will change if we end up locked down. But, in the quiet of the night, I admit to feeling a little terror about the girls. I've already had such a huge part of my life snatched from me. I can't bear to think about being left behind here if something were to happen to the girls. I hate being forced to think about death again when it has consumed my focus for so long. But, if this fucker COVID lingers or ends up being around for the long haul, it better take me over the girls. I could not handle the alternative.

# # #

Hindsight: As we are all aware, the nightmare of COVID is still with us as I edit this diary nearly a year after the pandemic began. More than half a million people have died. Millions of us are grieving without benefit of the symbols and rituals we have always utilized to mourn our dead. I don't know how we have lasted this long. I don't know when it will end. I only know we will all be forever changed by what has happened to us and how we've dealt with it.

# # #

30 months: My mother has been visiting (AKA living with me) the last five months. I met up with my brother, her normal caretaker, at the beach in New Jersey this summer and brought her back home with me. I'd made the beach house reservation in January, before there was any knowledge of the pandemic and how much of a disaster it would turn out to be. By May, we'd lost my aunt and a cousin to COVID and another aunt to a fall. But the rental company refused to refund my money, having already taken a bath on the spring rental season.

So, with rising COVID numbers and terror in our hearts, we all got tested before packing a ton of sanitizer, food and toilet paper and hit the road for a vacation we desperately needed, but everyone was afraid to take. Essentially, this vacation could best be summed up as locked down together in an expensive rental. The original plan was that my mother would stay with me for a couple months until my daughter's wedding in late September. My brother would then drive back down for the wedding and take Mom back with him.

Well, the pandemic blew up those plans pretty quickly. Two weeks after my mother was down here with me, my daughter and soon to be son-on-law had to decide whether the wedding could be held in September 2020. Like thousands of others have experienced since the pandemic started, the kids decided to kick the can on the wedding to NEXT September (yes, a year from now) since we couldn't safely gather last month. Hence, my current anxiety on just how long my mother will end up staying here with me. We're at five months and counting.

The jury is still out on whether this mother/daughter experience has been better or worse than living alone. In some ways, it has been good for me: we've gotten closer—from a mostly distant and impersonal relationship to one that is now warmer. She was not a terrible mother. Nor a great one. As an adult, I look back and acknowledge she was trapped in a terrible marriage to a selfish bastard. Viewing it that way, I can afford to extend her some slack. However, my mother took her bad marriage bitterness card and doubled down. Nothing was ever her responsibility. No broken promise to their three children. None of the weekly, knock-down, drag-out scream fests endured by us kids were *her* choice. It was always the lying, cheating jerk's fault. She lived for moments to not only deflect blame, but to bask in the glory of making damn sure everyone knew that her suffering was 100% his fault.

Now that we've gotten to know each other again, I imagine my mom presumes us to be kindred spirits. Bonded over our mutual losses. A poor, little widow—someone people should feel sorry for and take care of. That's the movie she plays for herself. She believes we are far more relatable than I would ever agree. One of our few conversations on the subject left me dwelling on how unbelievably different our situations truly are. One day this week we were talking about my worthless father, and she made the comment that my father's death was the "absolute best thing" that had ever happened to her.

Had my father been anything less than the soulless bastard he truly was, her comment could have hit as a double blow. She lost her husband, but I'd lost a father. Theoretically. Or the caricature of one. But since he really was both a terrible father and a terrible husband, I could somewhat relate to her comment.

What surprised me more than her comment was my reaction. My fleeting thought that I *wished* I lived in the comfort of her truth. I'd be sitting here now; decent job; able to pay my bills and most important, not experiencing the soul sucking grief that has abated only slightly in two and a half years and counting. Quickly appalled at myself, I pondered the trade-off that would have been required to be able to so casually despise my husband. To be both relieved and even—gleeful over his death.

That trade-off would have been far too high a price to pay. My thirty-six years of wonderful with Dan in trade for his far too early death and my immense suffering now? Or fifty-seven years wasted with a man she shared only an abject, poisonous loathing? Supreme indifference to each other, broken only by the daily volley of venom spewed at the prick she'd tied herself to. Too lazy to ever release him from the bonds of shared hatred. Too ensconced in their toxic battle to ever loosen her clutches and walk away.

My mother is now 87. Though somewhat mellowed by time, she is still a combination of bitterness and perpetual victimhood. She'd wished for my father's death for literal decades. My brothers and I grew up in the constant volley of accusations far beyond our kid-sized comprehension. Trapped in the no man's land between two opposing sides. One man so utterly full of himself, he couldn't possibly care about anyone else; and the other too invested in her own victimhood to ever want to do something about it except make him suffer as fiercely as she could. Her goal always, was winning the battle of ugly words and careless, offensive deeds. The three of us kids, trapped in our foxholes, long forgotten in the cold, damp trenches on their vast battlefield. If there was any taking care of to be done, we did it for ourselves.

I still remember her "celebrating" her twenty-fifth wedding anniversary. Specifically—*without* my dad. It was a hen party. Huge, flamboyant, gaudy celebration. She spent a fortune on a party where she could bathe in the glory of her misery. Twenty-five years wasted in a loveless, hate-filled marriage. There were gifts and everything. I enjoyed the cake, not quite understanding at age 15 what all the female outrage and fuss was about. Little did she know she'd have to endure another thirty-two years with him before he finally gifted her by dying. The gift she'd always wanted more than anything. Conveniently, my brothers and I "forgot" to celebrate their 50th. None of us could stomach the thought of it.

I'll take a question from the audience: How am I not completely fucked up? That's a question my surviving brother and I still seek to understand. Personally, I get asked that a lot by friends who learn of my history. Especially the friends who knew Dan and our relationship. Because our marriage was the epitome of normal. Of easygoing. Of love and comfort with each other. How did I overcome such an effed-up upbringing? I'm in the camp of belief that we end up one of two ways: just like our parents, repeating their mistakes or we do the opposite—moving as far away from their beliefs and examples as humanly possible. How did I end up so "normal"? We all know *normal* represents a space on a very long continuum. Who knows on which end I truly fall?

# # #

Halloween: People always grope to seek the deeper meaning when bad things happen. Not so much in good times. Then, we just say, 'oh I'm/we're so lucky'. For over two years now, I've tried to find some meaning in my grief. Some nugget of wisdom one can possibly unearth in moments of great pain. *He's in a better place. It was his time to go.* All the other platitudes the bereaved hear over and over from our well-meaning friends. But even now, after the worst thing that's ever happened to me; I find no real solace in any of the deeper meanings I can scrape up. Ever the pragmatist; all I can summon is that this terrible thing happened and now I'm stuck with it. I must carry on. I must figure out my new life moving forward.

Unlike the first time, when Dan and I did all of it together; this time around, I'm left with no joy in the process of discovery of what my new life entails. No hope that this will somehow start to feel better after a time. That I will grow comfortable with this new, exciting life. These uncharted waters. I will find happiness with whatever comes my way. When the reality is that I'll play the hand I've been dealt. Because that's all I'm left with. It's not as though I get to freeze time and never move forward. Whether it's kicking and wailing or not, time marches on.

So, I can play this hand in misery, or I can play it feeling numb. For now, numb allows a small respite from this perpetual emptiness. *Nothing* feels better than sadness and soul sucking grief. Numb is better than pain. The occasional fleeting smiles and traces of humor are better than not experiencing them. But it's still not a life I'd wish on anyone. It's just the life I happen to be stuck with.

32 months: Endurance Today's question: Who would I have become? I realized something today— it certainly took long enough. For those who met their partners in their twenties or thirties and married older, there was, I assume, a life component they experienced that I am clearly missing. I'm talking about those people who "had a life" before meeting their partner. In solely this aspect, I tend to think it is the slightest bit easier for them to fall back on a previous history or pattern when they face life-altering moments like a divorce, or the death of their spouse.

I'm absolutely not saying it's easier for those people to endure their loss. This isn't a pain contest. I'm just saying a "before" life offers clues to who you were Before You Met Them—meaning maybe you could still be that person again on the other side. For me, I was a teenager when I met Dan. We met when I was 18. Some of the enormous grief I've endured since his passing is over the fact that I don't know what my life should look like now. I didn't have a life before I met him. I was a kid from a troubled home and then, thankfully, I met Dan. End of story.

I have trouble imagining my fallback because I truly don't know what life would have looked like if I hadn't met him. Would I have become a strident, man-hating woman like my mother? A blame-everyone-else-for-my-problems person? Would I have been cowed enough to marry some domineering loser like my father who would have ruined my life? Note to self: I think I can safely rule this one out.

For some, my situation could be viewed as a clean slate. You can do anything at all, they might argue. For those who know better, being able to do *anything*—to choose from an endless list of possibilities is more likely to paralyze me than if I had to choose from say, a list of fifteen options. When everything is possible, how do you ever narrow down those options to make your choice?

At least if there'd been say, five years of "me" pre-Dan, I might know which direction I should be turning. But I was a shy, introverted, eldest daughter in an abusive family. I protected myself and younger sibs from verbal abuse and daily, ever-changing dysfunction. My life each day was about survival. Not living. Not joy. It was about not getting sidetracked. Not getting smacked or verbally abused or punished. It was about not getting trapped there. About not getting sucked into that dysfunctional vortex and drowning.

Like millions of people, I had to put myself through college. To do this, I worked three jobs, attending classes around all my jobs. Unlike most peoples' reasons for putting themselves through college, mine was meant to be punishment. Unlike my brothers, my father decided that as a female, I didn't really *need* an education. After a lifetime of hearing about college and the money he'd allegedly set aside for me, he pulled the rug out from under me on my sixteenth birthday.

In hindsight, I now believe it was payback for my threatening to call social services on him over the child-molester friend incident. Therefore, early in my senior year of high school, in the midst of his latest midlife crisis, Dad blew the meager amount he'd set aside in a savings account for my education. That was the year he bought my brothers matching, candy apple red Pontiac Fieros.

Months later, as I adjusted my college dreams according to my newfound poverty, my father was still angered by my independent mutiny. My persistence in wanting to escape from hell to attend literally *any* college. So, what does any determined, amoral father do? He moved the goal posts. Backing me into a corner on where I was "allowed" to attend college. At sixteen—how was I supposed to fight that? I lived under their shanty roof and I had no money, other than the $ 3.15 an hour I was pulling down at Burger King working 40 hours a week at night and on weekends. Later, I would replace fast food with a retail job, a travel agency and an office job that all together paid only slightly more.

According to my dad, I couldn't go anywhere that required me to live there. That would remove me from his control. Of course, with me having to pay my own way, living at school would have been a luxury out of the question. Maybe. I personally couldn't afford it. But buoying my hopes were the two full scholarships I'd been offered and three partial scholarships at schools I was desperate to attend. My dream had always been to attend Smith College in Northampton, MA. By the miracle of hard work and lots of studying, I got an acceptance letter. They'd offered me a ¾ scholarship. I would only need another 3-4 thousand a year to attend my dream school. A top tier academic school. My ticket out of hell. From Smith, I could meet normal people, possibly land an internship and parlay hard work and good fortune into a job with potential. I'd be able to move away. Anywhere that would take me far from my parents.

So, no matter what my father threw at me that year, I believed in my soul I would be able to make it happen without any assistance from him. I was still an optimist. A plucky little weed surviving in a crack in the sidewalk—needing little to survive. I'd already come so far, right? I'd already defied so many odds.

Until the day he moved the goal posts again. Not only would there be no purchase of books, sheets, toilet paper. Anything. But then my father announced there would be no form of transportation to get me to the school of my choice. He would not allow anyone to even drive me there. He forbade my mother to DRIVE me to college. There would be no help whatsoever to deliver me to any college I chose. My mother, of course, went along with his irrational demand—because "I can't control him". Looking back with forty years of hindsight, I believe she was also experiencing a gut level relief. That I'd be trapped, too. I was her buffer. Her sounding board. My being there made it easier on her.

So, at age sixteen, I was forced to turn down full scholarships at two universities and partial scholarships at three more — because

I didn't know how to adequately explain to an admissions officer that I would not be able to carry all my stuff on a bus (or train for two of the offers) and that I had parents who were refusing to help me. As in—they won't even drive me there. I was in the top three percent of my class academically. Yet, I was too humiliated and embarrassed to admit to a college admissions officer exactly what sort of dysfunctional hell I was living in. That I couldn't accept the full ride scholarship they were offering because it didn't include bus fare or money to ship my belongings.

My spirit broke the day I had to tell the recruiter at Smith that my answer was no. Her tone expressed utter disbelief that I was turning it down. But I didn't have any money. I didn't know how I would pay for the rest of it. I didn't know how I would get there on the day they told me to show up. And I didn't know how to tell her that.

Very late to the game, I frantically applied for loans in my own name (not knowing one scintilla of what I was doing as I completed FAFSA parent forms that were years beyond my comprehension). By then all the need-based scholarships were long gone at the local schools within driving distance. In the end, I took out high percentage loans instead of the low interest student loans everyone else landed. All to attend a local, adequate-but-nothing-special school that I could drive to. The school hadn't even been on my list. It wasn't a safety school. It wasn't anything to me. I hadn't visited the campus. I didn't even know what majors they offered. It was a school that bought me eight months to figure out how I would get there. If I had no transportation by then, I could take three buses and get to campus each day.

I ended up saving enough to be able to buy a shitty car to get me back and forth. When my father learned I'd saved just enough to buy the shitty car, he refused to go look at them with me, let alone pay a dime toward it. I went alone to the dealerships. For four more years, I was forced to remain living in my parents' home. The amount of the loans I received that first year? Turned out to be *exactly* what I needed to get me through my first year at Smith. My total loans after four years at no-name-university? The amount I would have paid for the four years at Smith with their partial scholarship (assuming I'd continued receiving aid). It's still heartbreaking when I think about it.

I wept, I'm sure, for several days after that latest ultimatum. Then something inside me just hardened into a tight, angry knot. Hatred for my father. Disillusionment for my disappointment. To be so close to the dream of an incredible education—and ultimately the escape it would provide me—and I'd failed to achieve it. I'd dug my way out of prison only to be caught at the fence line. Yanked off the barbed wire by snarling guard dogs.

Depression and a sort of grim finality set in. Over the terrible luck to be born into such an awful family. Friends with far less academic interest and drastically lower grades were going to great schools, paid for by their completely normal parents. Parents that had filled out the FAFSA and secured loans—instead of making their sixteen-year-old do it. That year—the year of supposed escape—I was left behind. Too smart for where I was going, but too poor and too powerless to change my situation.

That angry knot in my chest also contained resolve and determination. No matter what school I ended up attending, I vowed that my bastard father would never pull me under again. I would make it out of that family, or I would die trying.

I'm sure when Dan met me at school the following semester, he wondered where on earth I'd come from. A quick-to-anger, self-reliant, workaholic pessimist to his wide-eyed, optimistic, faith-based, kind-hearted kid from a very poor but loving and supportive family. It's truly a wonder that I found such a phenomenal person in Dan. He made all the misery of my upbringing lessen in importance. He loosened the knot that had formed inside me. When I look back on those years, I would always spin it as destiny that I met him at the school I'd never wanted to attend. Maybe that was the cosmic reason for me getting trapped there. So Dan could find me.

I would never, ever want to trade any of the years I shared with Dan. But now, as I face this blankness inside myself, it stems from a place where I morphed from the abused introvert to a fully loved and appreciated partner. Zero to sixty. Our life was a wonderful time of growing together, struggling to put myself through college, then juggling low paying jobs and too many bills; raising kids and working together to solve problems. Taking our one vacation a year that we could barely afford. I had hobbies and he had hobbies that were done occasionally when we found time for ourselves.

In many ways, I feel as though before Dan, I was a blank slate that never got scribbled on; never got smudged or erased. Aside from the terrible upbringing and all the obstacles my father set in my path— who was I actually meant to be? Now that it's just me, I'm having trouble figuring it all out. I have no reference point when I look back. Maybe having nothing to fall back on IS the plan. We should always be looking forward, right? But the confused part of me wonders—will I just know at some point what I want to do? What I'm meant to do?

Complicating my personal issues, the pandemic has us all living in suspended animation. We can't go anywhere nor do anything, anyway. So, I just keep puttering along. The horrific "new normal" everyone has been stressing over the last nine months is pretty much old hat to me. I've been living in my "new normal" hellscape for over two years now. The pandemic hasn't changed much for me. Aside from increasing my isolation—which stings after I've spent two years crawling out of the hole I've been in; otherwise not much else has changed (for me). Finally seeing light at the end of my dark tunnel, only to be plunged back into a new loneliness has been hard to take. But going in to work each day has provided the sense of structure that saved me after Dan died. As long as I don't catch COVID from driving in to my office, I assume that structure will propel me thru the pandemic as well.

# # #

November, 2020: Hope My mother has finally returned home after five months of living here with me. The drive to get her back to my brother was arduous during the spiking pandemic numbers. Eight hours roundtrip with no stops at all. Trapped in the car, hoping I won't need to pee before I can get safely back home. When I returned, I made a beeline for the bathroom. And started guzzling water to rehydrate. You don't realize how much you actually drink during a day until you deny yourself the opportunity to do so. It's like when the doctor reminds you not to drink liquids after midnight before a surgery. I never actually drink liquids after midnight. I'm usually asleep long before then. But when someone says not to do it—all of a sudden, I start getting thirsty.

After drinking several glasses of water, I began the clean-up process for a room that hadn't been accessible for nearly six months. While doing so, I discovered that my mom had left several items of clothing for when she returns *next* summer. My mother is 87 years old. I smiled as I threw the stack into the washing machine. That she just automatically assumes there *will be* a next year. Age. A pandemic. Nothing stops her, really. She truly believes she'll be back here next summer. While I admire her courage, I wonder how she can be so certain.

It's like those people who stockpile soap or paper towels or canned goods (I'm talking pre-pandemic). In the back of their minds, are they thinking "nothing can happen to me for the next three months . . . because I have nine bars of soap already on hand"? Or the people who assume nothing can happen to us because we have pets to feed. I probably used to think that way. When the reality always has been that we could be dead tomorrow. The bars of soap would sit in the cabinet, untouched. Still in their cellophane. Gathering dust until the end of time. Or until they're eventually donated to a homeless shelter. Dan died with no warning. Along with all his clothes, there were four pairs of sneakers he'd never worn. Size 15. Whenever he found shoes in his size, he would buy them and stockpile them because large sizes like that are hard to find.

As I scooped my mother's still warm clothes from the dryer and placed them back in the drawer, I found myself wondering whether I should start viewing my life more like my mother does. Instead, I worry about my cats starving to death in my absence, slowly giving up hope in the days after I disappear from the planet. No one to jump in and pick up the torch and carry on. No one to keep the ship righted. No one to remember that you were even here. I'm not sure I'll ever be able to share my mother's confidence when I lost someone in such a shocking, sudden way. So early. So unfairly.

I grieve for those who, each day now are losing family members to this virus. Who will have to carry on without their loved ones. Who will endure what I have endured. Who will have to find their new normal when their old normal was simply snatched from them without warning. Those who are now grieving the loss of their person to a virus that, until last year didn't even exist in our imagination. Half a million victims and still counting. The ripple effect of grieving loved ones must count in the millions. We have become and will continue to be a global community of grievers. All of us working through the cataclysm of loss and the material detritus our loved ones have left behind. A Mount Rushmore of stockpiled soap. I'm still working through Dan's. After two and a half years, I have three bars of soap to go before I can return to the brands I prefer. I wonder at that point if I'll remember what they were.

# # #

December, 2020: Not Unhappiness Throughout time, we have pondered the question 'what would make me happy?' New Year's Eve was the time I would typically succumb to the pressure of that question for maybe 30 minutes while we waited for our Chinese takeout to arrive. I always felt indulgent when my mind drifted in that direction. I had a pretty great life. Nearly three years into this new journey through Suckville, I am compelled to revisit it once again.

2.9 years into this new life, the question I now ask myself is the slightly adjusted "what would make me *not unhappy?*" I am beginning to suspect that what truly made me happy was the *absence* of unhappiness. My life before Dan died consisted of 13,140 days of routine, sometimes boring sameness of work and home; husband and kids; laughing and chatting; Chores and relaxing.

We all know this passage of time. The day-to-day juggle of too many life balls in the air at once. I wasn't unhappy during any of that time. I'm not saying there weren't days when I wanted to get in the car, drive off – and never return. Fewer days when I wanted to drive off a bridge and a tiny number (countable on two hands—and maybe one foot) of days when I wondered why I'd ever gotten married at all. Back then, I wouldn't have claimed my life to be joyous—but it was my life, and it was a good one and I appreciated it.

I like routine. I liked my husband, along with loving him. I liked our structure. I gained comfort from our routine together. The glorious set-your-watch-by-it sameness. It was reliable. Sturdy. Dependable. But on the rare days I paused to analyze whether I was happy enough – on New Year's Eve—what I believe I was stretching for was some measure of joy I assumed must be missing. Because isn't there always more? Shouldn't we always be reaching for more? For joy? JOY—in all caps. With lots of exclamations!! Shouldn't we be giddy with it? Drunk with it? Routine doesn't translate to joy, does it?

Isn't there an obligation for all of us to check our pulse? To see whether it's elevated enough? Should I be questing for more? It made for some tense moments on New Year's Eve. Then, thankfully, I'd eat too much Chinese food, drink a bit of champagne and fall asleep, usually before midnight. We'd both wake up on the couch and drag ourselves up to bed. The next day, I'd wake up and revert to my old standby—that beloved routine, relieved to set aside such a bothersome question until the next New Year's Eve.

Now, I've come to realize that your routine—my routine. Our routine IS happiness. The sameness. The elemental comfort level you derive with another person—the person you haven't quite taken for granted, but you've maybe forgotten how mission critical he is to helping you achieve the things you are so fond of. To me, that is the definition of happiness. There is no mystery to it.

If you remove that key component, I can see why people revisit the happiness question so frequently. I never felt the urge to question it more often than annually. Perhaps it was laziness on my part, or just being too tired most of the time. It certainly wasn't FOMO. We were not FOMO kind of people. If I had ever said FOMO to Dan, he would have done two things: 1) asked what FOMO meant and 2) laughed me out of the room.

Now, I look back and realize I didn't question happiness very often because I actually HAD IT. And thankfully, we both appreciated it. If I feared anything back then, it would have been the fleeting worry of losing that happiness "someday"— before I was prepared for it—as though you could possibly prepare for the death of a spouse. My greatest fear is what actually came true. That comforting happiness is gone. Never to return.

Now, I'm left with trying to achieve some new level of routine I can live with. That's my FOMO now. My fear of never experiencing a comforting, smile-inducing routine again. In this horrible time of COVID, that is what we should all be taking stock of this New Year's Eve. How long will each of us continue to have the awesomely normal situation we're in? People who haven't experienced loss yet should be fearing the day their beautiful routine life blows apart. Because it will likely occur on a day when you're "happy" and not thinking about what you already have. Believe me, that day will be the worst of your life. Tonight, on New Year's Eve as I watch Anderson Cooper be overtaken with his annual attack of giggles, this is what I'll be wishing for in 2021. An end to the virus. A modicum of happiness. A routine that brings a little comfort and makes me smile again.

# # #

Three years and one week: Acceptance? Today the sun is shining. Iris is cuddled in my lap. Ginger purrs contentedly on the arm of the couch. (And yes, we are watching a Hallmark mystery together). It is a rare lazy Sunday I am allowing myself to indulge in. Or maybe I've finally reached the point where I'm okay without a frenzy of activity to fill my every waking moment. At this specific moment, I realize I am not exactly happy, but I am content. As the three-year marker has just past, I can recognize this as a noticeable improvement over the past 36 months. I am not foolish enough to believe I will wake up this way every day going forward, but I'm appreciative that I woke up this way today. Today hints at what is possible for me as I move forward. It hints at possibilities. I am going to grasp these feelings and hold on tight to them.

I write this with a sense of relief and a glimmer of hope for all of us. It feels today as though I'm finally exiting the forest I've been wandering for three years. As much as I assumed I would languish, curled in a fetal position and eventually die in there, it still hasn't happened yet. Instead, I've emerged, permanently scarred from the journey. I've been weakened by it and toughened by it. I will never be the same person I was before I entered that forest. That person did die. But a new clone of me has obstinately persevered through the darkness. Turns out I'm a weed, after all. A scrappy little troublemaker that will find that crack in the sidewalk to survive in. Apparently, I will continue to fight for water and light.

Today I can acknowledge the sun. One day, you will, too. For me, I plan to embrace this newfound awareness. All we have left is to move forward. It has been a lonely journey and will likely continue to be so, but one thing I discovered as I stumbled along this path is that there are grooves to it. The trail is dusty and flattened from the countless others who have trod before us. There are signs along the way if we're looking for them. Signs of encouragement. Friends and strangers who offer guidance and support that can help us move forward. And there is our own instinct. Though we will always be on this path, there will eventually be patches of light after the terrifying darkness. If we enter another forest, hopefully we'll know better how to find our way out again. To those who are still thrashing through the brambles, still in the dark, I hope I've left some breadcrumbs for you to follow. It would be a shame if all our collective agony cannot be offered up to assist someone else.

# # #

Hindsight/Conclusion: I still haven't found all the answers. I am relieved to inform you that life has gradually, incrementally gotten better. It's a "better" that is somewhat like weight loss. Most change happens so gradually it's hard to notice a difference. You're so close to the situation you don't realize you're actually doing better. Until you zip up those pants that used to be tight and they are now magically a bit looser. Or someone compliments you and you realize the sit-ups must be paying off.

As far as grief goes, I'm equating it to the increments of time. When Dan died, I was suffering every minute of every day with an intensity I pray I will never experience again. Gradually, that suffering has lessened. I'm better now than I was three years and two weeks ago. Am I happy? No. Do I know what happy will look like once it arrives? No. Maybe happiness will be as incremental as weight loss. An occasional smile. Laughing at a sitcom on TV. Losing myself in a book for an hour. Am I content? I'm grateful to say I've started to re-experience contentment—some days.

So, my search continues. For meaning. For peace. For answers to my question of "what's next?" If you've read this far, that's probably not the answer you were hoping for. Me, either. But it's the answer I'm living with for now.

This book took a long time to write. Each word was so painful. It took even longer to edit. I dreaded going back and reading what I'd written at the worst time of my life. I put off the editing for months. Each essay forced me to relive the anguish I experienced in the moment. Re-reading and editing made me cry all over again. Isn't it natural I would want to avoid it? Then the pandemic hit.

But all along, I've been unable to shake the feeling that I was *supposed to* do this. To capture the agony of this process. I think about the "message" the medium relayed from Dan through my daughter. "You need to tell your story". There is an arrogance to that statement. Who am I to tell *my* story? I'm just one of millions who have suffered a loss. But, if it really was a directive from Dan, who, in life was my greatest cheerleader, then who am I to question it? He knew me better than anyone.

Looking back makes me cry. But reading my earliest entries also forces me to acknowledge how far I've come. I have to admit I am better now than I was when Dan died. This knowledge both betrays and comforts me. I can't help wondering if my tears are tinged with relief. I've made it this far. I'm still here. I'm functional. When he died, I believed I would not be able to survive this loss. In some ways, I prayed I wouldn't survive it.

As I'm typing and weeping, Ginger is trying to climb in my lap to comfort me. I didn't have a Ginger when this nightmare started. I didn't have Iris, my sweet, loving basket-case who now sleeps cuddled next to my leg each night. When Dan died, I was completely alone. I'm not alone now.

Sparks of my former personality continue to make occasional appearances. I smile more now. I think my message, if there is one buried in this slogging mess, is that we have to take comfort in whatever will get us through another day. Hopefully, that is isn't drinking too much or medicating the pain away. But if we can find something—anything that gives us hope, we should latch onto it. Anything that allows us to smile each day is healing in that moment. It could be a pet. It could be your job. Volunteering. Your friends. The neighbor who checks in with you to make sure you're okay. The hobby that frees your mind even for an hour. The painting or puzzle or book you read. It may not be enough, but it's something. Maybe you need to write about your own journey through the woods.

Selfishly, I knew I had to complete this diary. If only to be able to move on. I have been unable to write anything fiction since Dan died. I have let my readers down for nearly three years now. Unable to focus. Unable to think creatively. Unable at times to even sit still. I'm giving myself a pass, due to overwhelming grief, but even I know I can't use that excuse forever.

So, I am hopeful once this project is finally completed, I will be able to return to my stories, if only to rediscover the pleasure and frustration of the creative process. For the ability to lose myself in a story and forget my real life if only for a while. Isn't that what we do as readers? Forget our own troubles to be absorbed in the trials of a fictional character? Anyway, that's what I hope for. Peace and eventual happiness. I hope the same for you. Best wishes on your journey. You are not alone.

# # #

Resources:

This list below is a compilation of sources I have discovered along the way. Books I have read, websites and Facebook groups I have both lurked and taken part in. It is by no means definitive. You should conduct your own exploration of local resources, too.

Group Therapy/Group Activities: Once the pandemic is finally behind us, I highly recommend a group-type therapy. I found mine through a MeetUp group for widows. MeetUp (post pandemic) can be a great way to find other people who are interested in the same things you are. It was a way to forge ahead with a semblance of a social life when I was floundering in the early days and desperately lonely.

You may also find widows groups through your local hospice, local funeral homes may have information; churches, hospitals, bereavement counselors may have information on groups forming. Ultimately, my widows' group has been a great source of strength to me.

Books You May Find Helpful:

Second Firsts – A Step-by-Step Guide to Life after Loss by Christina Rasmussen. I loved this book.

Bearing the Unbearable: Love, Loss and the Heartbreaking Path of Grief by Joanne Cacciatore, PhD.

The Year of Magical Thinking by Joan Didion

It's OK That You're Not OK – Meeting Grief and Loss in a Culture that Doesn't Understand by Megan Devine

Grief Day by Day- Simple Practices and Daily Guidance for Living with Loss by Jan Warner

When Bad Things Happen to Good People by Harold Kushner (Though this book carried a message of acceptance, I don't think I was ready to read it when I did.)

Answers About the Afterlife- A Private Investigator's 15 Year Research Unlocks the Mysteries of Life after Death by Bob Olson (read this if you are interested in visiting a medium. It was fascinating. It also offered an explanation of the afterlife energy force that I appreciated.)

Good Grief – Heal Your Soul, Honor Your Loved Ones and Learn to Live Again by Theresa Caputo. (This was an easy and interesting read, but my probably unpopular opinion is that it felt as though she glossed over the pain of loss, not willfully, but because she's only ever lost a grandparent (to date of the book printing). She may be able to contact the deceased, but I didn't feel reading this book that she had the capacity to understand the immense suffering of a widow/widower). To me this book felt too surface-y.

The Ultimate Retirement Guide for 50+ Winning Strategies to Make Your Money Last a Lifetime by Suze Orman

Websites:

Widow 411 – tons of resources for widows. I have consulted this site numerous times.

Option B

ModernWidowsClub.org – a wonderful site with tabs on widowed parenting, support groups and events by US state and region; book clubs, art groups, a travel club for widows, etc.

CNBC.com Money 101

Wiserwomen.org – this site is fantastic for all things financial. Help with finding state and federal resources for widows, elderly, child and elder care. A wealth of information resides here. I am so glad I stumbled across it.

Facebook Groups:

Surviving the Death of a Spouse Support Group

Modern Widows Club

Option B Coping with Grief Support Group

Grief Beyond Belief (for non-religious support)

For Widows Only

Dr. Joanne Cacciatore

Widowed Women Over 50 – Moving Forward

Hope After Loss For Widows and Widowers

Healing Hearts: A Support Group for Widows and Widowers

Late Night Widows and Widowers

Widows and Widowers- Healing, Support and Education

All Things Afterlife

Traveling Widow

Widows' Friend

Fans of Hallmark Channel (just seeing if you're paying attention!)

American Widows Project for military widows

Finance-related Facebook groups:

Women On FIRE (Women's Personal Finance)

Choose FI

Beware Romance Scams (for those interested in dating)

Money Diaries

Suze Orman

Getting Organized: Your Starter List: This is not the be all-end all, but it may be helpful in getting you started on the path of getting organized and it will help your loved ones find everything when/if you're incapable of showing them. This is just a starting point to help you begin the process of summarizing your life on paper. You should add, remove as you see fit. The most important thing to do is start. The second most important thing is to keep it updated. Third: tell someone you trust where they can find it when the time comes.

Sample Summary of Your Accounts; Life Policies; Passwords: Think of this as your life summarized on paper. Help your family access your accounts, pay bills/shut down accounts. Every time you update, change the revision date and print/save the new one.

Your Home: Try to be thorough so you capture as much information as possible: Think of the questions someone would have as they enter your home. For instance, do you have an alarm system? Does anyone know how to disarm it? Where's your wi-fi password located? Do you have cloud storage? Do you receive mail at home or at a P.O. Box? Do you have pets? Where re their vet records? What do they eat? Who would you want to care for them.?

Legal records: Where are your legal documents stored? Your will. Your Power of Attorney and medical directive. Birth, death, marriage certificates, social security card, children's vaccination records, passport. Spell it out and be specific with locations. *"My will and power of attorney, medical directive, etc. are located in the safe in the upstairs hall closet."* Try to make it as easy as possible on your family. Trust me, they will thank you.

Life Insurance: This could be a policy through work or a stand-alone policy. List the company; the website; phone number. Policy number; Value; Beneficiaries and their contact information. If it is a stand-alone policy, describe it. Example: *A 20 year term policy in force through 12/31/37.*

Long Term Care: Company name; address; phone; website; policy number; beneficiaries if there is a life insurance component. Try to add some detail here because these policies are complicated and your family may be trying to pay for your care.. Example: *Policy pays for LTC for up to 6 years @ $ 3200 per month. Pays for in-home care. Indexed for inflation at 3% per year.* May have a life insurance component or a cash out benefit. If it does, explain that too.

401k; 403b; Pensions; Investment Accounts: List all the accounts you have. You probably have a 401k or 403b plan through work; IRAs from former jobs or that you opened individually. Are they Roth (post-tax)? Or pre-tax accounts. You may possibly have a pension. For each account, list the provider; website; phone number. Account number for each; who is the beneficiary on each account and their contact information. ID and passwords to access each account. You could add in the value of each account. For pensions, if you are receiving payment – include some information. For instance, it may have an original value that if not earned out by death would be payable to someone else upon your death. Example: *Pension $ 1200 per month paid on the 1st of the month for my lifetime. Routes to checking acct. Original value: $ 100,000.*

Checking/Savings/Money Market: List all banks where you have accounts; website and phone number; Account numbers; type of account; ID and password; balances.

PayPal/Venmo: ID and passwords; where does the money route to?

Health Savings Account: Provider; website; phone number; your ID and password; balance in the account. Beneficiaries.

Vehicles: Create a file that includes vehicle titles; loan information, etc. If you have a Department of Motor Vehicles account, write down the username and password. Do you have an EZ Pass? Leave account information so this account can be shut down. Car insurance: list the carrier; website; ID and password and the account where it is paid from. If you have a car loan – list the website; account number; username; password and any loan information you have. Example: *five-year loan at 2,9%. $ 300 per month from checking account. Paid on the 5th of the month. Loan payoff date 12/22.*

Bill Pay Online: utilities; power, gas, electric, cell phone, cable, etc. List all sites; account number; username and password, where is the payment drawn from. *Example: electric bill; 5th of the month; paid from checking account.*

Mortgage; home equity; installment loans; credit cards; health insurance/Medicare; media accounts like Hulu, Netflix, etc. List all sites; username and password; amount paid, day of the month and from which account.

Email Accounts: Do you have more than one? List accounts along with username and password for each.

Social Media Accounts: Facebook, Instagram, Twitter, Pinterest, etc. so your family can shut down your accounts. List all your accounts with username and password.

Add your own ideas here:

Dedication

In loving memory of my Dan. This book is dedicated to all the widows and widowers who are struggling to get through each day. Don't give up the fight. You are not alone. I also offer my undying gratitude to the courageous and encouraging women of my widows' group: LIFT: We are the Ladies Inspiring the Future Together. I am truly honored to know them. Some of the countless people who carried me through these early years: my precious girls and their wonderful boys. The rocks in my life who have stood by me so many times: D & M; T & J; E & D; my fortieth anniversary pals- we still need to get that trip in! My blessed neighbor P who saved my sanity on a nightly basis. Heartfelt thanks to every one of them and to so many others who have supported me through my grief.

Donations

A portion of the proceeds of this book will be going to two wonderful non-profits. The first is Safe Harbor Shelter to support the beautiful, strong women who struggle with domestic or partner violence. You can assist them at safeharborshelter.com[1]. The second will be to my local humane society in my ongoing effort to thank them for allowing me to foster my sweet girls, Ginger and Iris. I am a proud and eternally grateful foster failure.

---

1. http://safeharborshelter.com/

About Lauren Giordano

Typically, I write fiction. I have two series in contemporary romance and romantic suspense. Thankfully, these books are nothing like The Heartbroken Diaries. If you're ever ready for something lighter, you can learn about my upcoming releases by following me at www.laurengiordanoauthor.com[1]. Follow Lauren on Facebook[2] or Twitter[3]. Let's all hope for happy reading going forward.

1. http://www.laurengiordanoauthor.com

2. https://www.facebook.com/laurengiordanowrites/

3. https://twitter.com/lgiordanowrites

Don't miss out!

Visit the website below and you can sign up to receive emails whenever Lauren Giordano publishes a new book. There's no charge and no obligation.

https://books2read.com/r/B-A-AGEF-ZCCPB

BOOKS 2 READ

Connecting independent readers to independent writers.

www.ingramcontent.com/pod-product-compliance
Ingram Content Group UK Ltd.
Pitfield, Milton Keynes, MK11 3LW, UK
UKHW022002190726
13853UKWH00004B/1686

9 798201 617318